THE USBORNE BEGINNER'S COOKBOOK

Fiona Watt

Designed by Mary Cartwright
Illustrated by Kim Lane
Photography by Howard Allman

Recipes by Roz Denny, Julia Kirby-Jones
and Catherine Atkinson
Food preparation by Ricky Turner and Lizzie Harris
Cover Illustration by Christyan Fox

Contents

COOKING
FOR BEGINNERS

Before you begin

Before you begin to cook any of the
recipes in this book, read through the
pages at the beginning of each section.
They will give you tips about cooking.

Equipment

Always read through the recipe
you are planning to make before
you start to cook. This is to
make sure that you have
all the equipment you
will need.

Sharp
knife

Serrated
knife

Slotted
spoon

Wooden
spoon

Colander   Potato
            peeler

Strainer

Kitchen
scissors

Brush

Garlic press

Spatula

Measuring
jug

Large
mixing
bowl

Grater

Chopping
board

Baking
sheet

Oven mitts

Your oven

Arrange the racks in your oven
before you turn it on to the heat it
says. If you have a convection
oven, read its instruction
book and reduce the heat,
or the cooking time,
by the amount the
book suggests.

Ingredients

Before you start to cook, make sure that you have all the ingredients in the list at the beginning of the recipe. Ingredients are shown by weight and by using cups and spoons. Those shown by weight are generally sold that way.

Using caution

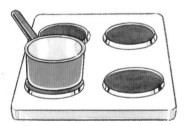

When you are using a saucepan or frying pan, always make sure that the handle is turned to the side of your stove top.

Be careful that you don't touch anything hot. Wear oven mitts whenever you put dishes into, or take them out, of your oven.

Don't leave your kitchen while you're cooking on the stove burners. Always turn off your oven, burners, or broiler when you finish.

Measuring with a spoon

If you don't have special measuring spoons, you can use regular spoons. Measure the ingredient as a level spoonful, not heaped up above the edge of the spoon, unless you are told to.

Soup spoon

A tablespoon

Teaspoon

A level spoon

A heaped spoon

Cooking hints

These two pages explain the cooking words and skills which appear in the recipes in this book. Read through them before you start to cook.

Breaking an egg

Crack the shell by tapping an egg sharply on the rim of a cup or a bowl. Push your thumbs into the crack and pull the shell apart.

Sifting

1. You sift an ingredient to get rid of any lumps. Place your strainer over a large bowl and spoon in the correct amount.

2. Lift the strainer slightly and shake it from side to side. You may need to use a spoon to push the last bit through the strainer.

Adding salt and pepper

Try adding a pinch of salt and three or four 'twists' of a peppermill.

In some recipes you will find that it says to add some salt and pepper. The amount you add depends on your own taste.

Beating a mixture

Before you begin to beat a mixture, put a damp dishcloth under your bowl. This stops the bowl from slipping as you beat.

Briskly stir the ingredients together with a wooden spoon or whisk, until they make a smooth, creamy mixture.

Making stock

Crumble a bouillon cube into a measuring cup, then pour boiling water into the cup. Stir it with a spoon until the cube dissolves.

Peeling potatoes

Wash your potatoes in cold water, first.

Hold a potato in one hand, then scrape a potato peeler toward you again and again to remove all the skin.

Grating cheese

Cut a piece of cheese which weighs more than you need. Grate some, then weigh the grated cheese. Grate more if you need to.

A garlic bulb *A clove of garlic*

Some of the recipes in this book include garlic. A clove of garlic is one of the sections of a whole bulb.

Preparing garlic

1. To remove a clove of garlic from the bulb, squeeze and twist the bulb until you split the outer layers of skin.

2. Slice a small piece off the top and bottom of the clove, then peel off its skin. The garlic is now ready to crush.

Using a garlic press

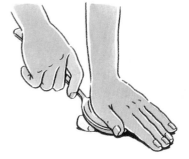

1. Put a clove of garlic inside a garlic press, like this. Close the press and squeeze the handles together tightly.

2. Run the blade of a knife over the holes on the press, to scrape off any crushed garlic which is still sticking to it.

If you don't have a garlic press, put a clove of garlic under the back of a spoon. Push down firmly on the clove several times.

Chopping an onion

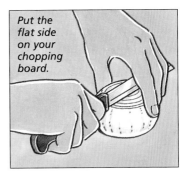

Put the flat side on your chopping board.

1. Put the onion onto a chopping board. Use a vegetable knife to cut off the top and the bottom. Be careful as you cut.

2. Run your knife around one side to slice the skin. Lift a piece of the skin at the cut, then peel the rest of it off the onion.

3. Hold the onion like this and cut it in half. Put the cut side onto the chopping board and chop each half as finely as you can.

Tomato and mozzarella salad

Serves 4

4 large ripe tomatoes
4 tablespoons of olive oil
salt and ground black pepper
10oz. mozzarella cheese
8 large fresh basil leaves

Use a serrated knife.

Core

1. Cut the tomatoes in half and cut the core out of each one. Lay each half on its flat side and slice them as finely as you can.

2. Arrange the tomatoes on four plates. Trickle a tablespoon of oil over each one. Sprinkle on a little salt and some black pepper.

3. If your mozzarella is in a bag full of liquid, slit the bag and pour the liquid away. Cut the mozzarella into thin slices.

4. Lay the slices of mozzarella among the tomatoes. Tear the basil leaves into thin strips and sprinkle them on.

5. Cover the plates with plastic food wrap and leave them in your refrigerator for about 30 minutes, then serve.

Summer salad

Serves 4

1 small crispy lettuce
half a cucumber
1 large carrot
3 green onions
a tub of alfalfa sprouts

For the dressing:
3 tablespoons of olive oil
1 tablespoon of white wine vinegar
1 teaspoon of clear honey
a pinch of dried mixed herbs
a pinch of salt and ground black pepper

1. Cut the end of the stalk off the lettuce. Pull the leaves off, wash and tear into bite-sized pieces. Put them into a large bowl.

2. Cut the cucumber in half lengthwise. Scrape out the seeds with a teaspoon. Cut each half into thin slices.

3. Use a potato peeler to peel the carrot. Grate it by rubbing it down, again and again, on the biggest holes on a grater.

4. Add the cucumber and carrot to the lettuce. Cut the roots and tops off the green onions. Slice them into ¾ inch pieces.

5. Add the onions to the lettuce. Use kitchen scissors to snip the sprouts from the tub. Add them to the bowl.

6. Put all the ingredients for the dressing into a jelly jar. Screw on its lid and shake it well. Pour the dressing over the salad.

Leek and potato soup

Serves 4

2 medium potatoes
2 medium leeks
2 tablespoons butter
1 tablespoon of cooking oil
1 vegetable bouillon cube
dried bouquet garni
1¼ cups of milk
small handful of fresh parsley
salt and ground black pepper

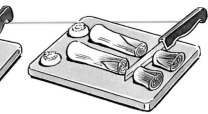

1. Peel the potatoes with a potato peeler. Cut them into small chunks, then put them into a large saucepan.

2. Cut the roots and the dark green tops off the leeks. Slice through the outside layer and peel it off each leek.

Stir the vegetables occasionally.

3. Wash the leeks thoroughly under cold, running water. Make sure that there is no dirt left in the layers.

4. Cut across the leeks so that you get ½inch slices. Put the slices into the pan and add the butter and oil.

5. Turn on the heat and slowly melt the butter. When it starts to sizzle, put a lid on the pan and turn the heat down low.

Stir until the bouillon cube dissolves.

6. Let the vegetables cook gently for ten minutes. Shake the pan occasionally to stop it from sticking, but don't lift the lid.

7. Meanwhile, boil some water. Put the bouillon cube into a measuring cup. Pour in 4 cups of boiling water and stir it.

8. When the vegetables are cooked, carefully pour in the stock. Add a pinch of bouquet garni, the milk and a little salt and pepper.

Chopping parsley

Stir it occasionally.

9. Turn up the heat and bring the mixture to a boil. Then, turn the heat down so that the mixture is bubbling gently.

10. Let the soup cook for 15 minutes, until the leeks and potatoes are soft. Ladle it into bowls and sprinkle it with chopped parsley.

Put the parsley into a mug. Use scissors to snip the parsley into fine pieces. It is easier than using a knife.

Cheesy beef burgers

Serves 4

1lb. lean ground beef
2 tablespoons light soy sauce
1 teaspoon dried bouquet garni
ground black pepper
1½oz. Cheddar cheese
sunflower oil

Make sure that your hands are clean.

1. Remove the broiler pan and rack from your broiler and put it to one side. Turn your broiler on to its highest setting.

2. Put the ground beef into a bowl. Break it up with a fork. Add the soy sauce, herbs and two 'twists' of black pepper (see page 4).

3. Mix the ingredients well and divide it in four. Squeeze each lump of mixture into a round, flat shape (see tip, right).

Press the cheese into the middle.

4. Cut the cheese into four cubes. Press a cube into each burger. Push the mixture over to cover the cheese.

You could serve your burgers with oven fries and salad.

You could serve your burgers in brown or white buns with lettuce and slices of tomato. Add a little mayonnaise too, if you like.

5. Fold a paper towel several times and pour a little oil onto it. Wipe it across the rack of your broiler pan.

Space the burgers out evenly on the broiler rack.

6. Use a spatula to lift the burgers onto the broiler rack. Turn the heat down to medium and cook the burgers for seven minutes.

7. After seven minutes, turn the burgers over, by sliding a spatula under each one and holding the top with a fork.

8. Cook the burgers for seven minutes more. Check that they do not become too brown. Turn the heat down a little if they are.

9. Press a fork on a burger to test it. If you like medium-cooked burgers they will feel springy. Well-done ones feel firm.

Tip: shaping burgers

Dip your hands in clean, cold water to stop the mixture from sticking to your hands when you shape it.

Creamy fish pie

Serves 4

1lb. 2oz. of boneless, skinless white
    fish fillet (e.g. cod or haddock)
1¾ cups milk
bouquet garni
salt and ground black pepper

4 medium potatoes
2 tomatoes
4 green onions
2 tablespoons of soft margarine
2 tablespoons of flour
1 cup frozen peas, defrosted

1. Put the fish into a
saucepan. Pour in the
milk, along with a pinch
of bouquet garni some
salt and black pepper.

*Watch the
pan in case
the milk
boils over.*

2. Bring the milk to a boil,
then turn the heat down
low so that it is bubbling
very gently. Cook it for
five minutes.

3. Take the pan off the
heat. Lift out the fish with
a spatula, but don't throw
away the milk. Leave the
fish to cool.

4. Meanwhile, peel the
potatoes. Cut them into
chunks. Put the chunks
into a pan and cover
them with cold water.

5. Add half a teaspoon of
salt and bring the water to
a boil. Turn down the heat
so that it bubbles gently.
Put a lid on the pan.

6. Cook the potatoes for
10-15 minutes until they
are soft. While they are
cooking, use a fork to
break the fish into flakes.

*Slice across
the onions.*

7. Cut the tomatoes into
small chunks. Cut the
roots and the green tops
off the green onions and
slice the onions finely.

8. When the potatoes are
cooked, drain them in a
colander over a sink. Put
the chunks back into the
pan, but not on any heat.

9. Crush the potato by
pressing a potato masher
down, again and again, on
the chunks. Do it until
there are no lumps left.

Mix it with a wooden spoon.

10. Add two tablespoons of milk from the fish pan and a tablespoon of butter, to the potato. Mix it well.

Turn the heat down to let it bubble gently.

11. Mix the flour with a little milk. Stir it into the milk, with a tablespoon of butter. Boil it, then let it bubble gently for one minute.

12. Add the fish, onion, peas and tomatoes. Cook for two minutes. Pour the mixture into an ovenproof dish. Turn on your broiler to medium.

Use a fork to make the top of the potato smooth.

13. Spoon the potato on top. Put the dish under the broiler. Cook it until the potato becomes golden. Serve it immediately.

Crunchy cheese omelette

For one person

1½ oz. mature Cheddar or Gruyère cheese
6 stems of fresh chives or 3 sprigs of fresh parsley
2 tablespoons of mini croutons
2 large eggs
salt and ground black pepper
2 teaspoons of olive oil

Look for mini croutons in the soup or snack section of a supermarket.

1. For the filling, grate the cheese on the coarse side of the grater (see page 4). Put the grated cheese into a small bowl.

2. Use kitchen scissors to snip the chives or parsley into the bowl. If you are using parsley, don't chop the thick part of the stalk.

3. Use your fingers or a knife to break the croutons into pieces, about the size of peas. Add them to the bowl and mix well.

You could add sliced tomato and basil instead of the croutons.

Page 4 shows you how to break an egg.

4. Break the eggs into another bowl. Add a tablespoon of water and a little salt and pepper. Beat them well.

You could serve your omelette with some lettuce.

The egg will set a little on the bottom.

Hold the pan handle in one hand.

5. Heat a small non-stick frying pan over a medium heat for a minute without anything in it. Then, add the oil.

6. Heat the oil for a few seconds. Carefully tilt the pan so that the oil coats the base of it. Pour in the egg and let it cook a little.

7. Use a non-metal spatula to pull the egg away from the side of the pan. Tip the pan to let runny egg flow into the space.

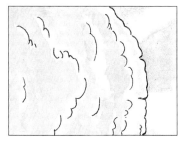

8. Keep pulling the omelette away from the side of the pan until all the runny egg is cooked. The top should still look creamy.

9. Spoon the filling all over the top. Tilt the pan at an angle and use a spatula to fold over one half of the omelette.

10. Leave the filling to cook for a few seconds. Turn off the heat. Slide the omelette onto a plate and eat it immediately.

Stuffed crêpes

Serves 4, makes about 12 crêpes

1 cup all-purpose flour
a pinch of salt
1 egg
sunflower oil
1¼ cups of milk

For the filling: 1 tablespoon of sunflower oil
14oz. lean ground beef or turkey
11oz. jar of tomato pasta sauce
5oz. of sour cream
2oz. grated Cheddar cheese

1. Put a strainer over a large mixing bowl. Pour in the flour and the salt. Shake the strainer until all the flour has fallen through.

Put a dishcloth under the bowl to stop it from slipping.

2. Press a whisk into the middle of the flour to make a deep hollow. Break an egg into a cup, then pour it into the hollow.

Use a whisk.

3. Add a tablespoon of oil and two tablespoons of milk. Beat the egg, oil and milk with some of the flour from around the hollow.

The mixture will make a smooth batter.

Brush the oil quickly over the bottom of the pan.

4. Add some more of the milk and beat it again. Continue to add some milk and beat it, until all the milk is mixed in.

5. Heat a small frying pan over medium heat for about a minute. Don't put anything into the pan at this point.

6. Put two tablespoons of oil into a cup. Fold a paper towel in half and roll it up. Dip one end into the oil and brush it over the pan.

The batter should sizzle.

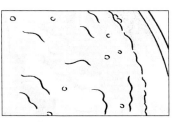

7. Put the batter next to your pan. Quickly add three tablespoons of batter. Swirl it all over the bottom by tipping the pan.

8. Put the pan flat on the heat and cook it until the batter turns pale and is lightly cooked. Small holes will also appear on top.

9. Loosen the edge of the crêpe and slide a spatula under it. Flip the crêpe over and cook it for half a minute more.

Make a stack of crêpes under the dish towel.

10. Slide the crêpe onto a plate then cover it with a clean dish towel. Repeat steps 6-11 until the batter is finished.

11. Heat a tablespoon of oil in a saucepan. Add the meat. Break it up with a wooden spoon and cook it until it is brown all over.

12. Stir the pasta sauce into the meat. Bring the pan to a boil then turn it down so that it bubbles gently. Cook for five minutes.

Fill each crêpe in the same way.

The dish will be hot.

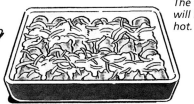

13. Lay a crêpe on a plate. Spoon on two tablespoons of mixture. Fold one side over the mixture, then roll it up.

14. Lay the crêpes, joint-side down in an ovenproof dish. Turn on your broiler. Spoon on the cream and sprinkle cheese on top.

15. Put the dish under the broiler. Leave it until the cheese starts to bubble and turns golden brown. Serve immediately.

Crusty bread 'pizzas'

Serves two

1 ciabatta bread,
or 1 thick French stick

For the topping; 1 onion
2 cloves of garlic
2 tablespoons of olive oil
14½oz. can of chopped tomatoes
half a teaspoon of dried bouquet garni
salt and ground black pepper
9oz. of mozzarella cheese
2 tablespoons of grated Parmesan cheese

Stir it once or twice.

1. Cut the top and bottom off the onion and peel it. Cut it in half and slice it. Peel the garlic cloves and crush them (see page 5).

2. Heat two tablespoons of oil in a frying pan. Gently cook the garlic and onion, for five minutes, or until they are soft.

3. Add the tomatoes, the herbs and some salt and pepper. Turn up the heat and bring the mixture to a boil.

You could put olives or slices of salami or ham on top of the cheese, before you cook them.

4. Turn the heat down to medium and let the topping cook for about ten minutes, or until most of the liquid has gone.

5. Take the pan off the heat. Leave the mixture to cool for 10-15 minutes. Turn your oven on to 400°F.

6. Put your bread onto a chopping board and carefully cut it in half lengthwise. Put each half onto a large baking sheet.

7. Spread each piece of bread with the topping. Slice the mozzarella cheese as finely as you can and lay the slices on top.

8. Sprinkle the Parmesan cheese on top. Bake the 'pizzas' for about 15 minutes or until the cheese is bubbling.

9. Take the baking sheet out of the oven and let the bread cool for five minutes. Cut each half into pieces, to make it easier to eat.

Try one with cheese, pepperoni and olives.

Cheesy spinach quiche

Serves 4

12oz. ready-made pie crust, thawed
   if frozen
8oz. fresh leaf spinach
1 onion
2 cloves of garlic
1 tablespoon of olive oil
2 cups grated Cheddar cheese

2 medium eggs
¾ cup half and half or whole milk
salt and ground black pepper

an 8 inch quiche pan or baking dish

Heat your oven to 325°F.

Make sure that your work surface is clean and dry.

1. Sprinkle a little flour on your work surface and onto a rolling pin. Shape the pie crust into a smooth, round ball.

2. Roll the pie crust, turn it in a quarter turn and roll it again. Keep on doing this until you get a circle about 10in. across.

3. Put your pan or dish onto a baking sheet. Roll the pie crust over the rolling pin then unroll the pie crust onto the dish.

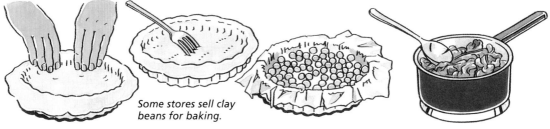

Some stores sell clay beans for baking.

4. Press the pie crust into the base and up the sides of the dish, without tearing it. Bring the pie crust over the rim of the dish.

5. Prick the base a few times with a fork. Press a sheet of foil into the dish, then fill the base with dried beans.

6. Put the crust into the refrigerator for half an hour. Turn on your oven. Wash the spinach and put the leaves into a large pan.

Press the water out of the spinach with the back of a spoon.

Wear oven mitts.

7. Cook the spinach for three minutes over medium heat. It wilts as it cooks. Drain it; press out the water. Leave it to cool.

8. Slice the onion and crush the garlic (see page 5). Put the oil into a pan. Cook the onion and garlic for five minutes, until they are soft.

9. When the pie crust has cooled, put it into the oven. Cook it for 15 minutes, then lift it out of the oven carefully.

10. Lift off the foil and the beans. Trim off the pie crust around the rim. Put the flan, uncovered, in the oven for five more minutes.

11. Turn your oven to 325°F. Spread the onion mixture over the crust. Cut up the spinach and add it too.

12. Sprinkle the cheese and a little salt and pepper on top of the spinach. Beat the eggs with the cream or milk, in a small bowl.

13. Pour the mixture over the filling. Put the quiche into the oven for about 30 minutes or until the top has set and is golden.

Pan-fried meat or fish

Serves 4

2 tablespoons of olive oil
either: 4 x 4oz. sirloin or rump steaks,
   or 4 skinless, boneless chicken breasts,
   or 4 x 4oz. skinless, boneless salmon fillets
2 sprigs of fresh parsley
salt and black pepper

1. If you are using chicken breasts, make two cuts on top of each one with a sharp knife. Put four plates in a warm place.

2. Put a non-stick frying pan onto a burner and turn it on to a high heat. Leave it for a minute without anything in it.

3. Pour the oil into the pan and brush it over the bottom. Add the pieces of steak, chicken or salmon. They will sizzle a little.

4. If you are cooking steak, cook the pieces on one side for two minutes, or for three to four minutes if you like them well done.

If chicken is cooked, the juices are clear, not pink.

If you are using chicken, cook the pieces for four to five minutes on one side. Chicken should always be well-cooked.

It makes it tastier if you let it stand.

For salmon, cook the pieces for about three minutes on one side. The fillets should be still be a little juicy and not dry.

5. When you have cooked the pieces on one side, turn the heat to medium. Turn them over and cook them for the same time again.

6. When the meat or fish is cooked, use a spatula to lift it onto the warm plates. Let them stand for few minutes.

This piece of chicken was cooked in a special skillet. The browned stripes are made by the ridges on the skillet.

7. Chop the parsley (see page 9) and sprinkle a little onto each piece. Serve the meat or fish with potatoes and a salad.

Lamb kebabs in pitta pockets

Serves 4

2 large lamb leg steaks, about 6 oz. each
1 clove of garlic
half a teaspoon of mild curry powder
1 tablespoon of oil
4 wooden kebab sticks
small head of leaf lettuce
half of a cucumber
2 tablespoons of natural yogurt
1 teaspoon of dried mint, or
1 tablespoon of fresh chopped mint
salt and ground black pepper
2 large pitta breads

You can squeeze some lemon juice onto the lamb before you serve it.

1. If there is a small bone in the middle of the lamb steaks, cut it out. Cut the meat into cubes, with sides about ¾ inch.

2. Peel and crush the garlic (see page 5). Put the garlic, curry powder, oil and a little salt and pepper into a bowl and mix well.

3. Add the meat into the bowl and stir it well. Cover the bowl with plastic foodwrap and leave it for half an hour.

Throw away the core of the lettuce.

4. Put the wooden sticks into a bowl of cold water and leave them to soak. This stops them from burning under the broiler.

5. Shread the lettuce by cutting across it and put it in a bowl. If you are using fresh mint, chop the leaves finely.

6. Cut the cucumber in half, then slice it finely. Mix the lettuce, yogurt, mint and cucumber, with a little salt and pepper.

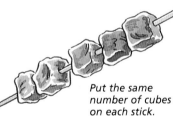  

Put the same number of cubes on each stick.

7. Turn your broiler on to medium. Dry the kebab sticks on a paper towel, then push the cubes of lamb onto them.

8. Put the kebabs onto the broiler rack and push it under your broiler. Cook the kebabs for five minutes, then turn them over.

9. Cook the kebabs for five minutes more. While they are cooking, cut the pitta bread in half across the middle, like this.

  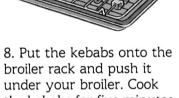

10. Put the kebabs on a plate. Put the pittas under the broiler for two minutes but turn off the heat. This will warm them through.

11. Run the tip of a knife along the cut edge of each pitta to open it up. Fill each one with some of the lettuce mixture.

12. Hold a kebab stick at one end and use a fork to slide the lamb off. Put some lamb into each pitta and eat immediately.

Vegetable stir fry

Serves 4

1 carrot
1 red or yellow pepper
2 zucchinis
4oz. snow peas
4 green onions
4oz. baby corn
1 clove of garlic
4oz. fresh bean sprouts
2-3 tablespoons of vegetable oil

For the sauce:
1 teaspoon of cornflour
1 tablespoon of light soy sauce
2 tablespoons of water
2 tablespoons of oil
a pinch of sugar

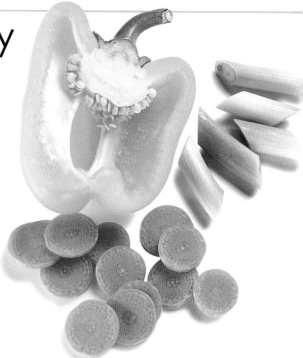

It's easiest to slice a pepper from the inside.

Cut the pieces about 2in. long.

1. Peel the carrot with a potato peeler. Cut off the top and bottom, then slice it into circles, as finely as you can.

2. Cut the pepper in half. Cut out the stalk and scrape out the seeds and white pieces inside. Cut it into thin slices.

3. Cut the ends off the zucchinis. Cut them in half lengthwise. Slice the halves into strips then cut them into shorter pieces.

4. Snip the ends off the snow peas using a pair of kitchen scissors. Then, cut each snow pea into smaller pieces, with a knife.

5. Cut the roots and the dark green ends off the green onions. Peel the outer layer off them, then slice them diagonally.

6. Cut the ends off the baby corn, then cut them in half lengthwise. Peel the clove of garlic and crush it (see page 5).

Stir quickly with a wooden spoon or spatula.

These vegetables were cooked in a special stir-fry pan, but you can use a large frying pan or a wok.

7. Put the cornflour into a cup and add a few drops of water. Mix it to make a paste. Stir in the rest of the sauce ingredients.

8. Heat two tablespoons of oil in a frying pan or wok. Add the carrot, pepper and zucchini to the pan. Cook them for three minutes.

Stir the vegetables as they cook.

9. Add the corn, garlic and onions. Cook them for a minute. Add the snow peas and bean sprouts. Cook the mixture for three minutes.

10. Stir the sauce in the cup then quickly pour it into the pan. Stir it to coat the vegetables and serve them immediately.

Pasta with fresh tomato sauce

Serves 4

For the sauce: 8 medium tomatoes
2 cloves of garlic
3 tablespoons of olive oil
half a teaspoon of sugar

12oz. dried pasta shapes
1 tablespoon of olive oil
salt and ground black pepper
12 fresh basil leaves

To serve: grated Parmesan cheese

Pasta shapes such as shells, twists or spirals are best for this recipe.

Use a slotted spoon.

1. Boil some water. Pull any stalks off the tomatoes. Use the tip of a knife to cut an 'X' on the bottom of each tomato.

2. Put the tomatoes into a heat-proof bowl. Carefully pour the boiling water over the tomatoes so that they are covered.

3. Leave the tomatoes for at least a minute. Fill another bowl with cold water, then spoon the tomatoes into it.

4. Lift the tomatoes out of the water. Use your fingers to peel off their skins, starting at the cuts you made.

5. Cut each tomato into quarters, then cut out the tough cores. Cut the fleshy part of each tomato into small pieces.

6. Peel the garlic and crush it (see page 5). Heat the oil in a large saucepan. Add the tomatoes, garlic and sugar and stir well.

7. Turn the heat to medium and cook the sauce for about five minutes. Stir it once or twice as it cooks.

8. While the sauce is cooking, fill a large pan with water and put it on to boil. Add a teaspoon of salt to the water.

9. When the water is boiling hard, add the pasta and stir it once or twice. Bring the pan back to a boil.

When you serve your pasta, sprinkle it with the grated Parmesan cheese.

10. Turn down the heat so the water is bubbling, but not too fiercely. Turn the heat under the sauce as low as it will go.

Drain the pasta in a colander over a sink.

11. Cook the pasta for the time it says on its package, then drain it. Rinse the pasta under cold water. Put it back into its pan.

Add a little salt and pepper too.

12. Add a tablespoon of oil to the pasta and stir in the sauce. Rip the basil leaves into pieces and stir them in. Serve immediately.

Shrimp and pepper curry

Serves 4

7oz. peeled, cooked shrimp
1 medium onion
1 clove of garlic
1 red or yellow pepper
2 tablespoons of oil
1 tablespoon of butter
1 tablespoon of mild curry powder
1¼ cups of basmati rice
1¾ cups of water
⅓ cup of shredded coconut
1 teaspoon of salt
1 cup of peas
freshly ground black pepper

1. If you are using frozen shrimp, spread them out on a plate. Leave them for two hours to defrost, then drain them in a colander.

2. Cut the ends off the onion, peel the onion and cut it in half. Slice each half finely then cut the slices into small pieces.

3. Peel the garlic clove and crush it (see page 5). Cut the red or yellow pepper in half. Cut out the seeds and the stalk.

Stir it occasionally.

4. Slice the pepper finely, then cut the slices into small pieces. Make them about the same size as the pieces of onion.

5. Heat the oil and butter gently in a large non-stick pan. Add the vegetables. Cook them on a medium heat for seven minutes.

6. Stir in the curry powder and add the rice. Add the coconut to the pan along with the water and salt.

Stir it once or twice.

7. Turn up the heat and bring the mixture to a boil. When it has boiled, turn the heat down so that it is bubbling gently.

8. Cover the pan and let it cook for ten minutes. Don't lift the lid while it is cooking as the steam in the pan cooks the rice.

Add a little black pepper too.

Stir it to separate the grains of rice.

9. Remove the lid carefully and stir in the shrimp and peas. Put the lid on the pan again and cook it for two to three minutes.

10. Take the pan off the heat and leave it, with the lid on, for five minutes. Stir the mixture with a fork and serve immediately.

Beef goulash with linguini

Serves 4

1 bouillon cube
1 onion
2 cloves of garlic
1 red or yellow pepper
1lb. braising beef
2 tablespoons of sunflower oil or olive oil
1 teaspoon of dried bouquet garni
1 tablespoon of paprika

1 tablespoon of wine vinegar
14½ oz. can of chopped tomatoes
7oz. linguini pasta
1 tablespoon of butter or soft margarine
5oz. sour cream
salt and ground black pepper

Heat your oven to 325°F.

Stir the meat as it cooks.

1. Make 1¼ cups of stock (see page 4). Cut the ends off the onion and peel off the skin. Cut it in half and slice it finely.

2. Peel and crush the garlic. Cut the pepper in half and remove the core and the seeds. Slice it finely. Turn on your oven.

3. Cut the meat into ½ inch chunks. Heat the oil in a frying pan over a medium heat. Add the meat and start to cook it.

Add a little salt and pepper too.

4. When the chunks of meat have browned all over, remove the meat with a slotted spoon and put it on a plate.

5. Put the onion, garlic and pepper into the pan. Stir them well and cook them for five minutes, until they are soft.

6. Sprinkle on the herbs and paprika. Put the meat back in the pan and stir it. Add the vinegar, tomatoes and the stock.

Wear oven mitts.

7. Bring the mixture to a boil, stirring it as it cooks. Once it has boiled, ladle it carefully into an oven-proof dish. Put a lid on the dish.

8. Put the dish into the oven for an hour. Take it out and stir it. Put the lid back and return it to the oven for half an hour.

9. About 20 minutes before the meat is ready, fill a large pan with water. Add a teaspoon of salt and bring the water to a boil.

10. Put the pasta into the water and bring back to a boil. Turn the heat down so that it isn't boiling too hard.

11. Cook the pasta for the time it says on its packet, then drain it in a colander. Spoon the butter onto the pasta and toss it.

12. Put the pasta onto four plates or bowls and put the meat onto top. Add some sour cream on top.

Cooking pasta

When you cook pasta, start measuring its cooking time from when the water boils again after adding the pasta.

This shows yellow egg linguini, but you could use green spinach linguini for this dish.

Roast chicken and vegetables

Serves 4

1 roasting chicken, about 4lbs., defrosted if frozen
2 tablespoons of oil
1 teaspoon of dried bouquet garni
1lb. new potatoes
2 medium onions, preferably red onions
1 red pepper
1 green or yellow pepper
2 tablespoons of sour cream
salt and ground black pepper

Heat your oven to 375°F.

Scrub the potatoes first if they are not clean.

1. Turn on your oven. Untie the legs of the chicken. Either pull off, or cut out, the fatty pads inside the chicken's body.

2. Place the chicken in a roasting pan. Rub a tablespoon of oil over the skin. Sprinkle it with herbs and some salt and pepper.

3. Put the potatoes into a clean plastic bag. Add a tablespoon of oil. Rub the potatoes so that they become coated with oil.

Don't cut the bottom off the onions.

4. Put the potatoes into the pan, around the chicken. Put the chicken into the oven and cook it for 45 minutes.

5. Meanwhile, cut the onions in quarters and peel off their skin. Cut the peppers into quarters and cut out the core and seeds.

6. Toss the onion and pepper pieces in the oily plastic bag. Add them to the pan when the chicken has cooked for 45 minutes.

7. So that the chicken browns evenly, put it back into the oven the other way around. Cook it for another 45 minutes.

8. After 45 minutes, scoop out the vegetables and put them in a serving dish. Put the dish into the oven, with the heat turned off.

9. Poke a knife into the meat beside a leg, to see if it is cooked. There should be no pink. If there is, cook it for five to ten more minutes.

Push a large spoon inside the chicken to lift it.

Pour the creamy juices over the pieces of chicken.

10. Lift up the chicken and hold it over the roasting pan and let the juices drip into it. Then put the chicken onto a plate.

11. Turn a burner onto a low heat and put the pan on top. Cook the juices for a minute, then stir in the sour cream.

12. Pull the legs and thighs off the chicken and cut the rest of the meat off with a sharp knife. Serve it with the vegetables.

Lemon and honey cheesecake

Serves 6

9oz. large graham cracker squares
4oz. butter
two 3oz. packages of lemon gelatin
    mix or 4½oz. package of
    concentrated gelatin
5 tablespoons of clear honey
10oz. heavy cream
7oz. sour cream
an 8in. quiche or pie pan with a loose
base. It should be about 1½in. deep.

Use the back of a spoon to press the crumbs.

1. Put the crackers into clean plastic bag. Seal the bag with a rubber band. Roll a rolling pin over the crackers to crush them.

2. Melt the butter in a saucepan over a low heat. Pour in the cracker crumbs from the bag and mix them with the butter.

3. Grease inside of the pan with some butter. Spread the crumbs over the bottom. Press them to make a firm base.

4. Chill the base in a refrigerator. Pour the gelatin mix into a measuring cup or cut up the concentrated gelatin.

5. Warm a tablespoon under a hot tap (see tip, below). Dry it and add five tablespoons of honey to the gelatin mix.

6. Pour 1¼ cups of boiling water into the cup. Stir the mixture well, until the gelatin dissolves. Leave the mixture to cool.

7. Meanwhile, put the cream into a large bowl. Use a wooden spoon to beat in the sour cream until it is smooth.

8. When the gelatin mixture is cool, pour it into the bowl with the creamy mixture. Beat it hard with a whisk to mix it well.

9. Pour the creamy mixture into the pan. Put it carefully into the refrigerator and leave it for about four hours to set.

Measuring honey

10. When the cheesecake is firm, lift it onto a can. Carefully press down on the sides of the pan to loosen the base.

11. Leave the cheesecake on the pan's base. Put it onto a plate and leave it in a fridge until you are ready to eat it.

Warm your spoon under a hot faucet before you dip it into a jar of honey. This makes it easier to measure.

Spiced apple crumble

Serves 4

3-4 eating apples
6 tablespoons of water
ground allspice
1 tablespoon of sugar

For the topping: 1 cup of all-purpose flour
1 cup of whole-wheat flour
¾ cup of sunflower margarine or butter
⅔ cup of light soft brown sugar

Heat your oven to 350°F.

1. Cut the apples in quarters, peel them. Cut out the cores. Cut the quarters into chunks. Put them in a medium casserole dish.

2. Add the water. Sprinkle the apples with a large pinch of allspice and a tablespoon of sugar. Turn on your oven.

3. Stir the two kinds of flour together in a bowl. Cut the margarine or butter into small pieces and add it to the flour.

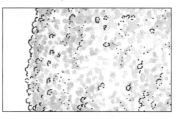

4. Wash your hands and dry them well. Rub in the margarine or butter into the flour using your fingers (see the tip, right).

5. When the mixture looks like coarse breadcrumbs, mix in the brown sugar. Mix it in with your fingers too.

6. Sprinkle the topping over the apple. Spread it out and smooth it with the back of a fork. Put the dish onto a baking sheet.

Wear oven mitts.

7. Bake the crumble for 45 minutes, until the top is golden. Turn the crumble around halfway through, so that it browns evenly.

8. Push the tip of a knife into a piece of apple. If it's not soft, put the crumble back into the oven for five more minutes.

9. Leave the crumble for at least five minutes to cool a little before you serve it. Serve it with ice cream.

You could use plums or blackberries instead of apples.

Rubbing in

Use a blunt knife to mix the pieces of margarine or butter. Stir and cut the flour until the pieces are coated with flour.

Rub the pieces between your fingertips. As you rub, lift the mixture up and let it drop. It will mix to look like breadcrumbs.

Strawberry trifle

Serves 4

1lb. fresh strawberries
4 short cakes (or sponge cake)
2 tablespoons of raspberry or strawberry jam
4 tablespoons of apple juice
1 small lemon
1¼ cups of heavy cream
3 tablespoons of milk
half a teaspoon of vanilla extract
2 tablespoons of sugar

1. Pull the stalks out of the strawberries. Try to pull them out with the white core attached. Use a small knife to help you.

Leave a few strawberries for the top of your trifle.

2. Cut most of the strawberries in half, or in quarters if they are big. Put the pieces into a medium-sized bowl.

3. Cut the cakes in half. Spread each half with jam then press them back together again. Cut the cakes into quarters.

Grate just the skin, not the white part beneath.

4. Put the pieces of cake on top of the strawberries and mix them gently. Trickle the apple juice over them.

5. Cover your bowl with plastic food wrap and put it into your refrigerator for about three hours. The cakes will turn soft.

6. Grate the yellow skin, or zest, from the lemon, using the medium holes on a grater. Use a knife to scrape off the zest.

Spread the cream with the back of a spoon.

7. When the cake mixture is nearly chilled, put the cream into a large bowl. Add the milk, lemon zest, vanilla and sugar.

8. Beat the mixture with a whisk until it forms soft peaks. If you beat it too much, it will become too solid to spread.

9. Lightly spread the creamy mixture over the cakes and strawberries. Put it in the refrigerator until you are ready to serve it.

Gooey chocolate fudge cake

Serves 6-8

2 teaspoons of sunflower oil
1¾ cups of self-rising flour
6 tablespoons of cocoa powder
2 teaspoons of baking powder
1½ cups of sunflower margarine
    (not low fat spread)
2¼ cups of soft brown sugar

2 teaspoons of vanilla extract
6 large eggs
5oz. dark baking chocolate
⅔ cup of milk
1½ cups of powdered sugar
¼ cup of butter

two 8 inch round cake pans

Heat your oven to 325°F.

Cut just inside the line you have drawn.

1. Turn on your oven. Put the cake pans onto wax paper and draw around them. Cut out the circles.

Use a pastry brush.

2. Brush sunflower oil over the inside of the pans. Put a paper circle inside each one and brush the top of it with oil.

3. Sift the flour, cocoa and baking powder into a bowl (see page 4). Put another large bowl onto a damp dishcloth.

Use a wooden spoon.

4. Put the margarine and sugar into the empty bowl and beat them until they are creamy. Add the vanilla and beat it again.

Don't forget to add a tablespoon of flour with each egg.

5. Crack one egg into a cup. Add it to the bowl with one tablespoon of flour. Beat it well. Repeat this with each egg.

This cake is best if it is eaten on the day you make it.

Change to a metal spoon.

6. Gently stir in the rest of the flour, moving the spoon in the shape of a number eight. This keeps the mixture light.

Spread the top level with a knife.

7. Put the mixture into the cake pans. Put them on the middle rack of the oven. Cook for 40 to 45 minutes. Test them (see page 45).

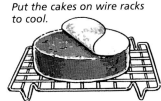

Put the cakes on wire racks to cool.

Use a heatproof bowl.

Run the knife around the edge again if it doesn't come out.

8. Wear oven mitts to lift the pans from the oven. Let them cool for five minutes, then run a knife around the sides of each pan.

9. Turn each pan upside down over a wire rack and shake it. The cakes should pop out. Peel off the paper and leave them to cool.

10. For the frosting, break the chocolate into a bowl. Add the milk and butter. Heat 2in. of water in a pan until it is just bubbling.

Put the cake on a plate.

11. Put the bowl in the pan. Stir the chocolate as it melts. When it has melted, add the sugar. Let it cool, then put it into a refrigerator.

12. Stir the frosting a few times while it is cooling. It will thicken. When it is like soft butter, take it out of the refrigerator.

13. Spread a third of the frosting on one cake. Put the other cake on top of it and cover the top and sides with your frosting.

Carrot cake

Serves 8-12 slices

a little oil for greasing
3 medium carrots
¾ cup margarine
1¼ cups light soft brown sugar
2 large eggs
1⅔ cups of self-rising flour
half a teaspoon of salt
2 teaspoons of ground cinnamon
2 teaspoons of baking powder

1 cup raisins
¾ cup chopped walnuts
2 tablespoons of milk

For the frosting: 7oz. cream cheese
1 tablespoon of lemon juice
2 cups powdered sugar
half a teaspoon of vanilla extract

an 8 inch round cake pan

Heat your oven to 350°F.

1. Put your cake pan onto a piece of wax paper and draw around it. Cut out the circle, just inside the line you have drawn.

2. Brush the sides and the base of pan with a little oil to grease it. Put the paper circle inside and brush this with oil, too.

3. Turn your oven on. Wash the carrots and cut off their tops. Grate them on the side of the grater with the biggest holes.

Put the bowl on a damp cloth.

4. Put the margarine into a saucepan and heat it slowly until it has just melted. Pour it into a large bowl.

5. Break the eggs into a small bowl and beat them. Stir the carrots and sugar into the margarine. Then, add the beaten eggs.

6. Put a strainer over the bowl. Shake the flour, salt, cinnamon and baking powder through the strainer, onto the mixture.

Push it in the middle.

7. Use a wooden spoon to beat the mixture, until it is smooth. Mix in the raisins and walnuts, then stir in the milk.

8. Spoon the mixture into the pan. Smooth the top with a spoon. Tap the pan on your work surface to make the mixture level.

9. Bake the cake for an hour. Test it by sticking a skewer into it. When it comes out it should have no mixture sticking to it.

10. Put the cake pan on a wire rack and leave it for ten minutes. Then, run a knife around the side of the cake.

11. Hold the rack on top of the pan and turn them both over. Shake the pan gently to get the cake out. Peel off the paper.

12. While the cake is cooling, sift the powdered sugar into a bowl. Add the cheese, lemon juice and vanilla.

Testing a cake

13. Beat the mixture well. When the cake has cooled completely, cut it in half. Spread one piece with half of the frosting.

14. Put the other half of the cake on top. Spread the top of it with frosting Make swirly patterns on it with a fork.

Push a skewer or a sharp knife into the middle of the cake. If the cake is cooked, it will come out clean.

Tasty cookies

Makes about 60 small cookies. This recipe shows you how to make fruit cookies. See the labels for other flavors.

1¾ cups all-purpose flour
quarter of a teaspoon of salt
2 teaspoons of baking powder
1 large egg
¾ cup butter
1 cup sugar
1 teaspoon of vanilla extract
1 orange and 1 lemon

Heat your oven to 400°F.

You can add all kinds of things to these cookies. Try 2oz. of chopped nuts instead of the orange and lemon zest.

1. Measure the butter and leave it for about an hour to soften. Sift the flour, salt and baking powder into a bowl (see page 4).

2. Break the egg into a cup. Beat it briskly with a fork, so that the yolk and the white are mixed well together.

3. Put the butter and sugar into another bowl and beat them until they are creamy. Stir in the egg and vanilla.

Scrape the zest off the grater with a knife.

4. Grate the skin, or zest, off the orange and lemon using the medium holes on your grater. Stir it into the creamy mixture.

5. Add the flour and stir it until you get a smooth dough. If the dough feels very soft, put it into your refrigerator for an hour.

Orange and lemon cookies.

6. Put a long piece of foil onto your work surface and scrape the dough onto it. Roll the dough to make a long sausage shape.

For chocolate cookies, add two tablespoons of cocoa powder. Sift it in with the flour.

Use four tablespoons of shredded coconut instead of the zest to make coconut cookies.

7. Wrap the foil around the dough and put it in your refrigerator for about an hour, until it becomes firm. Turn on your oven.

8. Take the dough out of the refrigerator and cut it into thin slices. You don't need to use all the dough at one time (see the tip).

Storing the dough

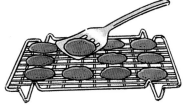

9. Spread out the slices of dough on a non-stick baking sheet. Bake them for about seven minutes, until they are golden.

10. Leave the cookies on the baking sheet for a minute. Using a spatula, slide them onto a wire rack to cool.

Wrap spare dough in foil. It will keep for about ten days in a refrigerator or up to six weeks in a freezer.

Useful information

• When you measure a liquid, look at the mark on your measuring cup at eye level, not from above.

• If you are measuring something like herbs, a liquid or salt in a spoon, don't hold the spoon over the mixture you are cooking, just in case some spills out of the spoon and into the mixture.

• If you're using a spoon to measure, make sure that the ingredient is level with the edge of the spoon and not heaped up.

• If you don't have a tablespoon, you can use a teaspoon instead. Three teaspoons is the same as one tablespoon.

Abbreviations commonly used

Here are some abbreviations which you may find in cook books.

tsp. - teaspoon
Tbsp. - tablespoon
c. - cup
pt. - pint
qt. - quart
oz. - ounce or ounces
lb. - pound or pounds
in. - inch or inches
min. - minute or minutes
hr. - hour or hours

Measuring ingredients

These conversions are equivalent measurements which are easy to use when you are cooking. They are not exact conversions.

3 teaspoons............................1 tablespoon
2 tablespoons........................ ⅛ cup
4 tablespoons........................ ¼ cup
5 tablespoons + 1 teaspoon.....⅓ cup

8 tablespoons.......................½ cup
12 tablespoons.......................¾ cup
16 tablespoons.......................1 cup
8 ounces................................1 cup
16 ounces...............................1 pound
2 cups.....................................1 pint
2 pints....................................1 quart
1 quart...................................4 cups

Substitutions for a missing ingredient

If the recipe calls for:-   use these ingredients instead:-

1 teaspoon dried herbs..................1 tablespoon fresh herbs
1 tablespoon prepared mustard....1 teaspoon dry mustard
1 crushed clove of garlic...............⅛ teaspoon garlic powder
1 cup sifted all purpose flour........1 cup plus 2 tablespoons sifted cake flour
1 cup sifted cake flour...................1 cup minus 2 tablespoons sifted all purpose flour
1 teaspoon baking powder...........¼ teaspoon baking soda, plus ½ teaspoon of
                                                            cream of tartar
1 square of chocolate (1oz.)..........3 or 4 tablespoons of cocoa, plus ½ tablespoon fat
1 tablespoon cornstarch................2 tablespoons of flour
1 cup buttermilk...........................stir 1 tablespoon of vinegar or lemon juice into 1
                                                            cup of sweet milk
¾ cup of cracker crumbs...............1 cup breadcrumbs
1 small fresh onion.......................1 tablespoon instant minced onion, rehydrated
3 medium bananas.......................1 cup of mashed bananas

PASTA & PIZZA

FOR BEGINNERS

Successful cooking

Before you cook any of the pasta or pizza recipes in this part of the book, read the tips on these two pages. Check that you have all the ingredients before your start. Don't worry if you haven't got the type or shape of pasta suggested in the recipe. Look on page 96, where you will find some alternative types to use.

Things to remember

The ingredients' lists shows some things which are measured by weight and others by cups. Generally, the things measured by weight are sold in that manner.

All the recipes tell you how long to cook the food, so follow these closely. Don't forget that if you have a convection oven look at its instruction book. Either shorten the cooking time or turn down the temperature by the amount it says.

Pizza bases

On pages 78-79 and 82-83, there are recipes for two different kinds of pizza bases. If you don't have time to make a base, many supermarkets sell ready-made bases. If you use one, just make the pizza topping from the recipe. You can also buy mixes for pizza bases.

Chopping onions

1. Put the onion onto a chopping board and use a vegetable knife to chop off the top and the roots. Be careful as you cut.

2. Slice through the papery outside skin. Use a fingernail to lift the skin at the slice then peel the rest of the skin away.

3. Cut the onion in half. Lay the flat side on your chopping board and, holding the onion firmly, slice it as finely as you can.

Garlic

A garlic bulb

A clove of garlic

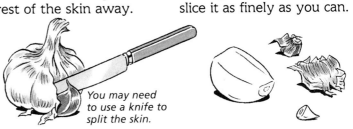

You may need to use a knife to split the skin.

If your recipe uses garlic, it will tell you how many cloves you will need. A clove is one part of a whole bulb of garlic.

1. Squeeze and twist the garlic bulb so that the the outer skin breaks. Pull a clove of garlic off the bottom of the stem.

2. Cut a small piece off the top and bottom of the clove, then peel off the skin. The clove is now ready to use.

Fresh or dried pasta?

You can use fresh or dried pasta for all the pasta recipes. You need a different amount depending on the type you use. See the ingredients' lists.

Mushrooms

Wash mushrooms before you use them and wipe them clean with a damp paper towel. Cut off the end of the stalk.

Mozzarella cheese

The pizza recipes use two types of mozzarella cheese. If it says to use 'mozzarella cheese', use the kind you buy in a plastic bag, surrounded by liquid. The other kind is written as 'grated mozzarella'. You can buy this ready-grated or as a large solid block.

Mozzarella cheese is soft and you can't grate it. Slit the bag you buy it in and pour away the liquid, before you slice it.

Grated mozzarella is firmer than the other kind.

Types of pasta

Each of the pasta recipes suggests a type of pasta for you to cook, but in most cases you can use any shape you like (see page 96). Many supermarkets sell lots of different kinds of fresh and dried pasta. If you see the words 'rigate' on a package of pasta, it just means that it has a ridged surface.

Tortellini (little twists). These are often stuffed with spinach, cheese or meat.

Linguini

Macaroni (tubes)

Ravioli. These are usually filled with meat but sometimes with vegetables, fish or cheese.

Fusilli (spirals)

Conchigliette (little shells)

Conchiglie giganti

Conchiglie (shells)

Penne (quills)

Egg noodles

Cooking pasta

The amount of time you need to cook pasta depends on its type and shape. Fresh pasta and long thin shapes cook more quickly than dried pasta or chunky shapes. Try not to overcook your pasta. It should be firm, not soggy.

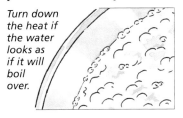

Make the pan three-quarters full.

Oil stops the pasta from sticking.

1. Fill a very large saucepan with water. Turn on the heat and bring the water to a boil. While the water is heating, measure your pasta, if necessary.

2. When the water is boiling and the surface looks as if it is 'rolling', not just bubbling, add a teaspoon of salt and a tablespoon of cooking oil.

3. Add the pasta to the pan and stir it to separate it. When you add the pasta the water will stop boiling. Turn up the heat and bring it to boiling again.

Turn down the heat if the water looks as if it will boil over.

4. Start to time your cooking, following the instructions on the package of pasta, from when the water boils with the pasta in it.

5. When the pasta has cooked for the correct time, hold a colander over a sink and pour the pasta into it. You may need help to hold the pan.

6. If you need to leave your pasta in a colander, put a little butter on it. Toss the pasta so that it is coated. Put a plate on top to keep it warm.

Cooking spaghetti

Vermicelli (little worms)

Red pasta has tomato in it and green pasta is made with spinach.

Spaghetti

Farfalle (pasta bows)

When you cook dried spaghetti, hold one end and gently press it into the water as it softens. Use a spoon to press the ends under the water.

Spaghetti alla carbonara

Serves 4

8-12oz spaghetti

For the sauce: 8oz. Canadian bacon or cooked ham
1 large onion
2 cloves of garlic
1 tablespoon of cooking oil
3 eggs
3 tablespoons of half and half cream
ground black pepper
½ cup of grated Parmesan cheese
¼ cup of butter
1 level tablespoon of chopped parsley

Add the spaghetti when the water is boiling.

Stir the onion and garlic as they are cooking.

1. Peel and chop the onion. Using scissors or a knife, cut the bacon into ½ inch strips. Peel and crush the garlic (see right).

2. Read the instructions on the package of spaghetti to find out how long it will take to cook. Add it to the boiling water.

3. Heat the oil gently in a frying pan. Add the onion and garlic, and cook them for about five minutes until they are soft.

Stir the mixture as it is cooking.

Turn off the heat when you drain the spaghetti.

4. Add the bacon or ham. If you are using bacon, cook it until it is brown and crispy. If you are using ham, cook it until it is hot.

5. Use a fork to beat the eggs, cream, a pinch of black pepper and most of the cheese to make a creamy mixture.

6. When the spaghetti is cooked, drain it then put it back into the pan. Add the butter and toss the spaghetti until it is coated.

The heat from the spaghetti cooks the egg.

7. Add the bacon, onion and garlic then stir in the cheesy mixture. Use a fork to toss the spaghetti quickly, until it is coated.

8. Put the spaghetti onto four plates or bowls. Sprinkle on the parsley and the rest of the cheese. Serve immediately.

Crushing garlic

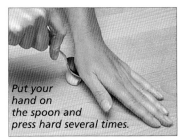

Put your hand on the spoon and press hard several times.

If you don't have a garlic press, put a clove of garlic on a chopping board. Put the back of a spoon onto it and press down.

Garlic mushroom pasta

Serves 4

14oz. dried fusilli (spirals),
   or 1 lb. fresh fusilli

For the sauce: 6 tablespoons of butter
1 lb. mushrooms
1 clove of garlic
salt and ground black pepper
8oz. container of sour cream

1. Fill a pan with water and bring it to a boil. Add your pasta to the pan and leave it cooking in the boiling water.

2. Slice the mushrooms thinly. Peel and crush the garlic. Gently melt the butter in a pan. Add the mushrooms and garlic.

3. Add a pinch of salt and pepper to the pan and cook over medium heat for about five minutes, stirring occasionally.

Serve your pasta on plates or in large, flat bowls.

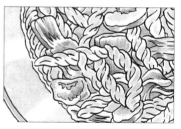

4. Drain the pasta and add it to the mushrooms. Add the sour cream and stir it until it is blended. Serve immediately.

This three-colored pasta is called 'tricolori fusilli'.

Spicy sausage pasta

Serves 4

14oz. dried conchiglie (shells),
   or 1 lb. fresh conchiglie

For the sauce: 2 tablespoons of olive oil
1 onion
1 clove of garlic
two 14½ oz. cans of chopped tomatoes
14oz. package of spicy, smoked sausage
1 tablespoon of chopped parsley

1. Peel the onion and slice it finely. Peel and crush the clove of garlic. Put the oil in a large pan and heat it gently.

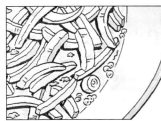

The sauce will reduce in amount.

2. Add the onion and garlic. Cook them for five minutes or until the onion is soft. Stir the mixture as it is cooking.

3. Drain the tomatoes and add them. Bring it to a boil then turn the heat down. Let the sauce bubble gently for 20 minutes.

You can always use salami if you don't like spicy food.

4. While the sauce is cooking, put a pan of water on to a boil. Cook the pasta following the instructions on its package.

5. Cut the ends off the sausages. Peel the papery skin off them, if necessary. Slice each sausage and add to the sauce.

6. Drain the pasta and divide it between four bowls or plates. Spoon the sauce on top and sprinkle with parsley.

Macaroni cheese

Serves 4

6oz. (1 cup) dried macaroni,
   or 7oz fresh macaroni

For the cheese sauce:
4 tablespoons margarine or butter
4 tablespoons flour
$2^2/_3$ cup of milk
1 teaspoon of mustard
6oz. Cheddar cheese, grated
salt and pepper

For the topping:
1oz. Cheddar cheese, grated

Heat your oven to 350°F.

Put the macaroni back into the pan after you have drained it.

Use a wooden spoon to stir.

1. Turn on your oven. Measure the macaroni. Read the instructions on its package and cook it for the time it says. Drain it.

2. To make the sauce, melt the margarine or butter in a pan over a low heat. Stir in the flour and cook it for one minute.

3. Take your pan off the heat and add a little milk. Stir it really well. Continue stirring in the rest of the milk, a little at a time.

Add a pinch of salt and pepper too.

4. Return your pan to the heat and start to bring it to a boil, stirring all the time. The sauce will stick if you don't stir it.

5. The sauce will begin to thicken. Let the sauce bubble for a minute then turn off the heat. Stir in the mustard and cheese.

6. Pour the sauce over the cooked macaroni. Stir it well so that the sauce coats all of the pieces of macaroni.

7. Dip a paper towel into some margarine and rub it inside an ovenproof dish to grease it. Pour in the cheesy macaroni.

8. Sprinkle grated cheese on top. Put the dish into the oven for about 25 minutes, until the top is golden brown.

Add the cheese to a sauce after you have turned off the heat and the sauce coats the back of your spoon when you lift it.

Penne with Bolognese sauce

Serves 4

1 lb. penne

For the sauce: 2 tablespoons of olive oil
2 pieces of Canadian bacon
1 onion
1 carrot
1 stick of celery
1 clove of garlic
8oz. lean hamburger
14½ oz. can of chopped tomatoes
2 tablespoons of tomato purée
1 beef or vegetable bouillon cube
1 teaspoon of dried basil
freshly ground black pepper

To serve: grated Parmesan cheese

1. Peel or scrape the carrot then grate it. Crush the garlic and chop the bacon, onion and celery finely. Heat the oil in a saucepan over a medium heat.

2. Add the bacon to the pan and cook for three or four minutes. Stir it occasionally. Add all the vegetables and cook them until they are soft.

3. Add the minced beef or lamb to the pan. Break up the meat with a spoon and cook it for six to eight minutes, or until the meat is brown all over.

4. Boil some water. Crumble the bouillon cube into a measuring jug and pour in ½ cup of water. Stir it well then add it to the meat.

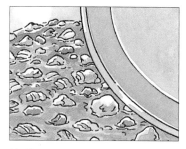

5. Pour in the tomatoes. Stir in the purée, basil, salt and pepper. Put a lid on. Let the sauce simmer for 30-40 minutes. Remove the lid halfway through.

6. As the sauce is cooking, stir it occasionally to stop it from sticking. It will become thicker and the amount of liquid will reduce.

7. About 15 minutes before the sauce is ready, boil a pan of water. Add the pasta and cook for the time it says on its package. Drain it and serve immediately.

Spoon the sauce over the hot penne and sprinkle with Parmesan cheese.

Making bouillon

1. Boil some water. Either cut up or crumble a bouillon cube and put it into a measuring cup.

2. Pour in the amount of water you need for your recipe. Stir it well until the bouillon cube dissolves.

Pasta with green vegetables

Serves 4

14oz. fresh linguini
2 tablespoons butter
4 green onions
½lb. (2 cups) broccoli
¼lb. (1 cup) thin green beans
¼lb. (1 cup) snow peas
1 zucchini
8oz. soft cheese spread with
garlic and herbs

*This green and yellow
linguini is known
as 'paglia e fieno'
(straw and hay).*

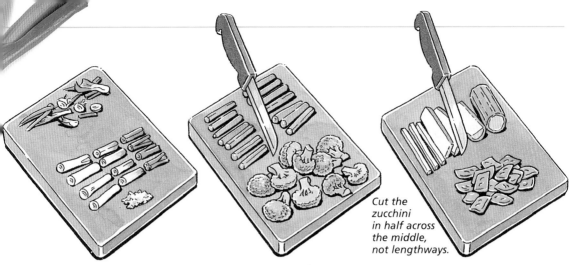

Cut the zucchini in half across the middle, not lengthways.

1. Chop the top and bottom off the green onions. Pull off the outer layer. Cut them into pieces, one inch long.

2. Use a knife to cut the curly ends off the broccoli stalks. Trim the ends off the green beans and cut them in half.

3. Trim the ends off the snow peas. Chop them in half. Cut the ends off the zucchini and cut it in half. Slice it into thin strips.

Cook on a low heat.

4. Fill a pan with water and boil it. Add the broccoli and beans and cook them for three minutes. Drain them.

5. Boil a pan of water for the pasta. Melt the butter in a frying pan. Add the onion, broccoli and beans. Cook them for five minutes.

6. Add the rest of the vegetables. Cook them for a further three minutes, stirring them occasionally.

Stir in a little milk if the sauce seems too thick.

Trimming vegetables

7. Cook the pasta for three minutes then drain it. Put it back into the pan and add the vegetables. Mix them well.

8. Add the cheese. Break it up with a spoon. Cook over a low heat until the cheese melts. Serve it immediately.

It's easier to use scissors rather than a knife to trim vegetables like beans or snow peas.

Ravioli with tomato sauce

Serves 4

14oz. fresh or dried ravioli
1 tablespoon of olive oil
1 onion
1 clove of garlic
two 14½oz. cans of chopped tomatoes
8 basil leaves
4oz. fresh, or 1 cup grated
   mozzarella cheese

1. Peel the onion and chop it finely. Peel and crush the garlic. Heat the oil in a saucepan and add the onion and garlic.

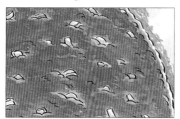

2. When the onion and garlic are soft, add some salt and pepper and the tomatoes. Let it bubble gently for 15 minutes.

This sauce is tasty with ravioli filled with meat, cheese or fish.

3. While the sauce is cooking, shred the cheese, if necessary. Cut the basil into thin strips. Boil a pan of water for the ravioli.

4. When the water for the pasta is boiling, add the ravioli and cook it, following the instructions on its package.

5. Just before the pasta is ready, add the cheese and basil to the sauce. Let the cheese melt a little then serve immediately.

Cheesy tortellini

Serves 4

14oz. fresh tortellini
4 tablespoons butter
4 tablespoons flour
2½ cups of milk
1 cup Cheddar or Gruyère cheese
1 heaped tablespoon of chopped parsley

Stir it as it cooks.

1. Grate the cheese. Boil a pan of water. Add the tortellini and cook them following the instructions on their package.

2. Mix the flour into the butter over low heat. Gradually add the milk, mixing well. Add the cheese and heat for five minutes.

3. Let the cheese sauce bubble gently for five minutes, stirring it from time to time. Add the chopped parsley.

4. Drain the pasta well and pour it into the cheese sauce. Stir it so that the pasta is coated then eat it immediately.

Spinach and ricotta pasta shells

Serves 4

16 conchiglie giganti (giant pasta shells)

For the filling: 1 onion
1 tablespoon of olive oil
1 clove of garlic
½lb. fresh spinach
8oz. ricotta cheese

For the tomato sauce: 1 onion
1 tablespoon of oil
1 clove of garlic
1 level tablespoon of tomato purée
2 level teaspoons of sugar
14½oz. can of chopped tomatoes
1 tablespoon of fresh chopped basil
salt and black pepper

To serve: grated Parmesan cheese

You can use 6oz of frozen spinach instead of fresh. Thaw it and drain it well. You don't need to add any water when you heat it at step 4.

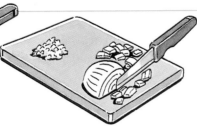

1. Fill a large pan with water and bring it to a boil. Add the pasta shells and cook them according to their package.

2. While the pasta is cooking, start to make the filling. Peel the onion and chop it very finely. Peel and crush the garlic.

3. Heat the oil and cook the onion and garlic until they are soft, but don't let them turn brown. Spoon them into a mixing bowl.

Stir it as it cooks.

4. Wash the spinach well. Put it into a large pan and cook it over medium heat for about two minutes.

5. Spoon the spinach into a colander. Press it with the back of a large spoon to squeeze out as much liquid as you can.

6. Put the spinach onto a chopping board and cut it up into small pieces. Use a fork to hold it as it will still be hot.

Toss the pasta in a little butter.

Make the sauce in a big, shallow pan.

7. When the shells are cooked, drain them in a colander and leave them to cool a little. Continue making the filling.

8. Put the spinach into the bowl along with the ricotta. Add a pinch of salt and pepper and mix everything together.

9. Make the tomato sauce following steps 2 to 5 on page 81. While the sauce is bubbling, begin to fill the pasta shells.

10. Hold the shell in one hand and use a teaspoon to fill each shell with some of the spinach and ricotta mixture.

11. When all the shells are filled, lay them, open-side up into the sauce. Heat them for 10-15 minutes with a lid on top.

12. Spoon four shells and some sauce onto each plate. Sprinkle them with Parmesan cheese and eat them immediately.

Chicken and bacon pasta

Serves 4

14oz. linguini
4 tablespoons of margarine or butter
14oz. boneless chicken
4 pieces of Canadian bacon
4oz. mushrooms
4 green onions
1 teaspoon of chopped parsley
2 level tablespoons of flour
1 cup of milk
4 heaped tablespoons of sour cream
salt and ground black pepper

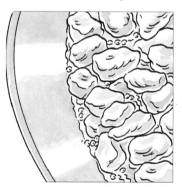

Cook over a low heat.

1. Cut the roots off each green onion. Trim the top and peel off the outer layer. Cut them into pieces, about an inch long.

2. Slice the mushrooms finely. Cut the bacon into small pieces. Fill a pan with water and put it on to boil.

3. Chop the chicken into small chunks. Melt the margarine or butter in another saucepan and stir in the chopped chicken.

4. Cook the chicken for five minutes until it loses its pinkness. Cut one piece in half to check that it's cooked completely.

5. Add the bacon to the chicken and cook for three minutes more. Then add the mushrooms and onions to the pan.

6. Cook the mixture for two minutes. Measure the milk into a cup and add the flour. Stir them well, blending until smooth.

The sauce will take about a minute to thicken.

7. Gradually add the milk to the mixture, stirring all the time. Continually stirring, simmer the sauce until it thickens.

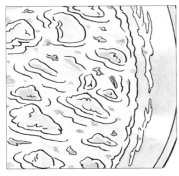

8. Add the sour cream and parsley. Put in a pinch of salt and pepper. Turn the heat as low as it will go while you cook the pasta.

9. Cook the pasta, following the time on its package. Drain it and put it back into its pan. Stir in the sauce. Eat it immediately.

Meatballs in tomato sauce

Makes 16 meatballs, serves 4

8oz. dried, or 12oz. fresh egg noodles

For the meatballs:
1lb. ground lean beef or lamb
2 level teaspoons of dried herbs
1 egg
1 tablespoon of flour
cooking oil, preferably olive oil

For the tomato sauce:
1 onion
1 clove of garlic
14½oz. can of chopped tomatoes
1 tablespoon of fresh chopped basil
1 tablespoon of tomato purée
salt and ground black pepper

Use a large mixing bowl.

1. Put the meat into a bowl and break it up with a fork. Crack the egg into a cup then add it, along with the mixed herbs and flour.

2. Wash your hands. Pick up some of the mixture and shape it into a ball, about the size of a table tennis ball. Make 15 more.

3. Heat three tablespoons of oil in a frying pan and add eight meatballs. Turn them often, until they are brown all over.

Always keep raw meat and cooked meat apart.

Stir the onion and garlic as they cook.

4. Put a paper towel onto a plate and put the browned meatballs onto it. Brown the other eight meatballs and put them on the plate.

5. Chop the onion and peel and crush the garlic. Heat a tablespoon of oil in a saucepan and fry them until they are soft.

6. Add the tomatoes, basil, purée and salt and pepper. Let it boil, then turn down the heat and bubble it gently for ten minutes.

You may have to look in the Oriental food section in your supermarket to find egg noodles. You could use spaghetti or vermicelli instead.

The oil prevents the noodles from sticking together.

Cook the noodles when the meatballs are ready.

7. Add the meatballs. Put a lid onto the pan and leave the sauce to bubble gently for 20 minutes, stirring occasionally.

8. While the meatballs are cooking, half-fill a pan with water and bring it to the boil. Add a tablespoon of oil to the water.

9. Add the noodles, let the water boil again, then simmer for the time it says on their package. Drain and serve with the meatballs.

Minestrone soup

Serves 4

4 pieces of Canadian bacon
2 sticks of celery
2 medium-sized potatoes
2 carrots
1 onion
1 leek
1 clove of garlic
1 tablespoon of cooking oil, preferably olive oil
1 tablespoon of tomato purée
2 bouillon cubes
4½ cups of water
1 teaspoon of mixed dried herbs
a quarter of a small dark green cabbage
½ cup small dried pasta shapes
½ cup frozen peas
salt and ground black pepper

To serve: 2oz. grated Parmesan cheese

Instead of using pasta shapes, you could use spaghetti broken into small pieces.

1. Use either a knife or a pair of scissors to cut the bacon into strips about ¾ inch wide.

2. Peel the potatoes and cut them in half. Cut each piece into ½ inch slices. Then cut the slices into cubes.

3. Wash the celery and the leek, and peel the carrots. Cut them all into thin slices. Peel the garlic. Peel the onion and slice it.

4. Heat the oil in a saucepan. Add the bacon. Cook it for a few minutes until it is brown then crush the garlic into the pan.

5. Add all the vegetables you have chopped and stir them well. Let them cook for five minutes, stirring them often.

6. Crumble the bouillon cube into a measuring jug and pour in 2¼ cups of boiling water. Add the tomato purée and stir well.

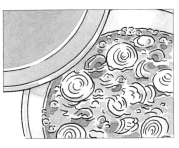

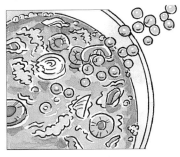

Cut out the stalk before you slice it.

7. Pour the stock mixture into the pan, Add another 2¼ cups of water, along with the herbs and a pinch of salt and pepper.

8. Turn up the heat so that the mixture boils. Put a lid on the pan and let the sauce bubble gently for about 20 minutes.

9. Meanwhile, remove the outer leaves from the quarter of cabbage and wash it. Cut it into very thin slices.

10. Add the cabbage and pasta to the pan and let it boil. Turn the heat down and cover it. Cook it for ten more minutes.

11. Add the peas to the pan and stir them in well. Let the soup cook for another two minutes until the peas have heated up.

12. Use a ladle to spoon the soup into four bowls. Sprinkle a little Parmesan cheese on top of the soup and eat it immediately.

Stir fry with vermicelli

Serves 4

6oz. dried vermicelli,
   or 8oz. fresh vermicelli
3 tablespoons of soy sauce
1 tablespoon of lemon juice
1 tablespoon of clear honey
1 inch piece of fresh ginger
10oz. boneless chicken breast
2 carrots
1 red pepper
1 clove of garlic
¼lb. snow peas
¼lb. baby corn
¼lb. mushrooms
4 green onions
1 tablespoon of sunflower oil
a vegetable bouillon cube

1. Cut the light brown skin off the piece of ginger. Cut the ginger into thin slices, then cut the slices into very thin strips.

2. Put the soy sauce, lemon juice and honey in a bowl. Add the pieces of ginger and stir them well. This is your marinade.

3. Cut the chicken into strips about ¾ inch wide. Add it to the marinade and stir well. Leave it for half an hour.

4. While the chicken is marinading, make 1¼ cups of bouillon (see page 61). Peel the carrots and cut them into thin 'sticks'.

See the tip on page 89.

5. Cut the ends off the pepper. Chop it in half and cut out the seeds. Slice the pepper into thin strips. Peel and crush the garlic.

6. Cut the stalks off the snow peas and slice the top off the corn. Cut them all in quarters. Slice the mushrooms.

Stir it all the time.

7. Trim the ends off the green onions, then cut them into pieces, about one inch long. Put a pan of water on to boil.

8. Heat the oil in a frying pan. When the oil is hot, add the garlic. Spoon in the chicken, leaving your marinade in the bowl.

9. Cook the chicken for five minutes. When all the pinkness has gone, add all the vegetables to the pan.

10. Stir the vegetables for three minutes. Pour in the bouillon and marinade and let it boil. Cook for two more minutes.

11. Add the vermicelli to the pan of boiling water. Boil it for three minutes, stirring occasionally then drain it well.

12. Add the vermicelli to the vegetables and stir it in. Leave the mixture for a minute then eat it immediately.

Tuna and tomato pasta salad

Serves 4

10oz. dried farfalle,
   or 12oz. fresh farfalle (bow pasta)
9oz. can of tuna
10 cherry tomatoes
⅓lb. thin green beans

For the dressing:
   1 cup of mayonnaise
   4 tablespoons of lemon juice
   salt and black pepper
   12 fresh chives

Toss the pasta with some butter.

1. Fill a large saucepan with water and bring it to a boil. Weigh the pasta and add it to the pan when it is boiling.

2. Cook the pasta following the instructions on its package. Pour the pasta into a colander to drain it. Leave it to cool.

3. Use kitchen scissors to snip the ends off the beans. Cut the beans in half. Put on a pan of water to boil.

4. When the water is boiling, add the beans and cook them for five minutes. Drain them and rinse them with cold water.

5. Open the can of tuna and drain away the liquid. Put it on a saucer and use a fork to break it up a little.

6. Put the pasta, beans, and tuna into a large bowl and mix them. Cut the tomatoes in half and add them to the bowl.

Instead of making a dressing, you could toss your salad in a ready-made one.

7. Put the mayonnaise and lemon juice into a bowl and add salt and pepper to taste. Use a fork to mix them together.

8. Pour the dressing over the pasta mixture. Use a fork to toss the mixture in the dressing so that it is covered.

9. Use kitchen scissors to snip the chives into small pieces and scatter them over the top. Spoon the salad onto plates or bowls.

Making a pizza base

This traditional pizza dough will make a round pizza 10 inches across, or a 14 x 10 inch rectangular one.

1½ cups of bread flour or all-purpose flour
1 teaspoon of salt
½oz. fresh yeast, or 1 teaspoon
    of rapid rise yeast
1 cup of warm water
1 tablespoon of olive oil
margarine for greasing

Cook your pizza on a large pizza pan or baking tray like this.

a 14 x 10 inch baking tray or a 10 inch pizza pan

It should take about 15 minutes to turn frothy.

1. If you are using fresh yeast, mix it with a little of the warm water. Leave it in a warm place until it becomes frothy.

If you are using rapid rise yeast, open the packet, measure the water and add a teaspoon of the yeast now.

2. Sift the flour and salt. Add the oil, yeast mixture and the rest of the warm water. Stir them well.

3. Continue stirring the mixture until you get a soft dough which doesn't stick to the sides of the bowl. Wash your hands.

4. Sprinkle flour onto a clean, dry work surface and knead the dough well until it is smooth and stretchy (see right).

5. Dip a paper towel into some margarine and rub the sides and bottom of a large bowl to grease it. Put the dough into the bowl.

The dough stretches as you push it.

1. Use the heels of both hands, or your knuckles, to push the dough away.

2. Fold the dough in half and turn it around. Push it away from you again.

3. Fold and turn the dough again. Push it away from you as you did before.

4. Continue folding, turning and pushing until the dough feels smooth and stretchy.

6. Cover the bowl with plastic foodwrap. Put it in a warm place for about 45 minutes, or until it has risen to twice its size.

7. Turn your oven on to 425ºF. Grease a baking tray or pizza pan with margarine. Rub it all over.

8. When the dough has risen, knead it again so that you burst all the large air bubbles in it. It won't take very long.

9. Put the dough onto your baking tray. Press it into the shape you want. Pinch up the edges. It's now ready for its topping.

Neapolitan pizza

Serves 6 - makes a rectangular pizza 13 x 9 inches

One traditional pizza base - see pages 78-79

For the tomato sauce: 1 tablespoon of olive oil
1 onion
1 clove of garlic
1 tablespoon of tomato purée
14½ oz. can of chopped tomatoes
1 level teaspoon of sugar
1 level tablespoon of fresh basil, chopped,
    or 2 teaspoons of dried basil
salt and ground black pepper

For the topping: 8oz. mozzarella cheese
2oz. can of anchovy fillets
1 tablespoon of fresh basil, chopped,
    or 2 teaspoons of dried basil
2oz. pitted and sliced black olives

Heat your oven to 425°F.

1. Turn on your oven. Follow pages 78-79 to make a pizza base. While the dough is rising, make the tomato sauce.

2. Chop the onion finely and crush the garlic. Put a tablespoon of oil into a medium-sized pan and heat it gently.

3. Add the onion to the pan and stir it occasionally for about five minutes until it has softened. Try not to let it turn brown.

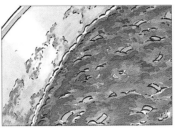

4. Add the garlic, tomato purée, tomatoes, sugar, basil and a pinch of salt and pepper. Stir it and let the mixture bubble gently.

5. Leave the sauce to cook for 20 minutes or until the sauce becomes thicker and the amount has reduced.

6. When your dough has risen, grease your baking tray with margarine. Place the dough in the middle of the tray.

7. Press the dough out with your fingers to make a rectangle about 13 x 9 inches. Pinch up the edges to make a rim.

8. Use a spoon to spread the tomato sauce all over the base. Slice the cheese thinly and lay the slices over the sauce.

9. Open the tin of anchovies carefully and drain out the oil. Cut each anchovy in half lengthwise.

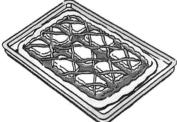

10. Lay the anchovies in diagonal lines across the pizza. Make lines the other way to make a crisscross pattern.

11. Sprinkle the basil all over the top then put an olive in the middle of each diamond shape made by the anchovies.

12. Put the pizza into the oven to bake for about 20 minutes, until the base is crisp and golden. Serve the pizza immediately.

Quick Margherita pizza

Makes one 12-inch round pizza
This recipe uses a scone base, rather than the
traditional base on pages 78-79.

For the scone base: 2 cups of self-rising flour
½ teaspoon of salt
2 tablespoons of cooking oil
¾ cup of water

For the topping: 1 tablespoon of cooking oil
1 onion
two 14½ oz. cans of plum tomatoes
1 teaspoon of mixed dried herbs
salt and ground black pepper
8oz. mozzarella cheese

Heat your oven to 400°F.

*Make sure that your
work surface is clean
and dry, first.*

1. To make the base, sift
the flour and salt into a
bowl. Add the oil and water.
Use a round-ended knife to
mix them to make dough.

2. Grease your pan with
margarine on a paper
towel. Sprinkle flour onto
your work surface. Knead
the dough (see page 79).

3. Rub a little flour onto a
rolling pin. Gently roll the
dough, turning between
each roll, into a circle
about 12 inches across.

*Pinch
up a rim
around
the edge.*

4. Carefully lift up one
edge of the dough and
slide the rolling pin under
it. Lift the dough onto
your pan or baking tray.

5. To make the topping,
peel the onion and chop it
finely. Gently heat the oil
and cook the onion until
it is soft.

6. While the onion is
cooking, open the can of
tomatoes and drain them
in a colander. Chop them
into small pieces.

This pizza is delicious eaten hot or cold.

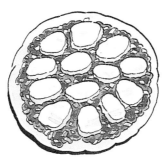

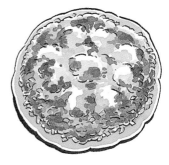

7. Add the tomatoes and herbs to the onion. Add a pinch of salt and pepper and cook the mixture for ten minutes.

8. Use a spoon to spread the topping over the base. Cut the cheese in thin slices then lay them all over the topping.

9. Bake your pizza in the oven for 25-30 minutes. The base will rise as it cooks and the cheese will turn golden.

Mini pizzas

Makes 4 pizzas six inches across

One traditional pizza base - see pages 78-79

For the toppings: 2 slices of ham lunchmeat
1 pineapple ring
1 tomato
4 large basil leaves
1oz. sliced pepperoni
2 small mushrooms
4-5 medium peeled, cooked shrimp
a small can of corn
4oz. (1⅓ cup) grated mozzarella cheese
1 jar of pizza sauce

Heat your oven to 425°F.

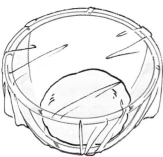

Cut the dough in half, then in half again.

1. Follow the steps on pages 78-79 to make the dough for the bases. When the dough has risen turn on your oven.

2. Put the dough on a floury work surface. Cut it into four and roll each piece into a six inch circle. Pinch up the edges.

3. Grease a baking sheet and put the dough circles onto it. Put a couple of tablespoons of pizza sauce on each base.

4. Cut the ham into small squares. Put these onto one of the bases. Chop up the pineapple ring and lay the pieces on the ham.

5. Slice the tomato finely. Lay them on another base. Cut the basil into small strips and sprinkle them on top.

Try different combinations of ingredients, such as tomato, shrimp and mushroom.

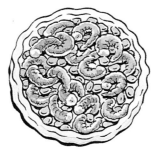

6. Lay the slices of pepperoni on the third base. Slice the mushrooms finely and spread them on top of the pepperoni.

7. Open the can of corn and drain it. Spread a tablespoon of corn over the base. Put the shrimp on top.

8. Sprinkle each of the pizzas with cheese. Bake them for 15-20 minutes until the bases and cheese are golden brown.

Chicago pizza pie

Makes one 9-inch deep pan pizza

For the dough: 1½ cups all-purpose flour
1 teaspoon of salt
½ teaspoon fresh yeast,
    or 1 envelope of rapid rise yeast
1 cup of warm water
1 tablespoon of oil

For the tomato sauce: ½ tablespoon of olive oil
    ½ onion, finely chopped
    1 clove of garlic
    8oz. can of chopped tomatoes
    1 teaspoon of dried basil
    salt and ground pepper

For the topping: 1 green pepper
    4 medium mushrooms
    sliced pepperoni
    6oz. grated mozzarella cheese

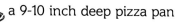

a 9-10 inch deep pizza pan

Heat your oven to 425°F.

1. Follow steps 1-8 on pages 78-79 to make the dough.

2. Put a little oil onto a paper towel and rub over the bottom and sides of the pan so that they are covered with oil.

3. Sprinkle a little flour onto your work surface and on your rolling pin. Roll the dough into a circle about the size of your pan.

4. Place the dough in the middle of the pan and press it out to the edges with your knuckles. Make it as even as you can.

5. Cover the pan with plastic foodwrap and leave it in a warm place for 20 minutes. It will rise a little bit more.

6. Turn on your oven. While the dough is rising, follow steps 2 to 5 on page 81 to make the tomato sauce.

See the tip on page 89 for cutting peppers.

7. Cut the ends off the pepper. Chop it in half and remove the seeds. Cut it into cubes. Slice the mushrooms thinly.

8. Spread the sauce over the dough. Lay the pepperoni, then the mushrooms and finally the green pepper, on top.

9. Sprinkle it with grated cheese and bake it for about 20-25 minutes until the dough is golden and has risen.

Shrimp pizza

Makes one 10-inch pizza

One traditional pizza base - see pages 78-79

For the tomato sauce: 1 tablespoon of olive oil
1 onion
1 clove of garlic
1 level tablespoon of tomato purée
14½ oz. can of chopped tomatoes
2 teaspoons sugar
1 tablespoon of chopped fresh basil
salt and freshly ground pepper

For the topping: half a red pepper
half a yellow or green pepper
6oz. peeled, cooked shrimp, thawed if frozen
1 level tablespoon of chopped parsley
1 tablespoon of olive oil

Heat your oven to 425°F.

Sprinkle flour on your work surface.

Pinch up a rim around the edge.

1. Follow pages 78-79 to make a pizza base. While the dough is rising, make a tomato sauce following steps 2 to 5 on page 81.

2. When your dough has risen and you have kneaded it again, roll the dough into a ten inch circle. Turn on your oven.

3. Dip a paper towel in margarine and rub it over a baking sheet to grease it. Lay the dough in the middle of the sheet.

4. Cut the seedy part out of the peppers. Slice them lengthways into strips. Try to cut them as finely as you can (see right).

5. Spread the tomato sauce over the base. Scatter the strips of pepper all over it. Sprinkle it with parsley.

6. If your shrimp were frozen, put them into a colander to drain away any liquid, then scatter them over the top.

You can buy lots of different colors of peppers. It doesn't matter which one you choose for this pizza.

Slicing peppers

7. Sprinkle on some salt and a little black pepper then carefully drizzle the oil from the spoon all over the top.

8. Put your pizza into the oven and bake it for about 20 minutes until the base is crisp and becomes golden brown.

When you slice a pepper, cut it in half then cut out the seeds. Slice it from the inside. It's easier than trying to pierce the skin.

Tomato and zucchini pizza

Makes one rectangular pizza 14 x 10 inches

One scone pizza base (see page 82)

For the topping: 1 tablespoon of olive oil
1 medium onion
1 level tablespoon of dried or fresh chopped basil
2 cloves of garlic
2 medium-sized beefsteak tomatoes
2 level tablespoons of pine nuts
1 small zucchini
salt and ground black pepper
8oz. grated mozzarella cheese

Heat your oven to 400°F.

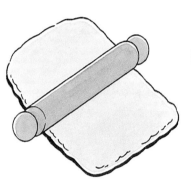

1. Turn on your oven before you make the dough. Follow steps 1-3 on page 82 to make a scone dough pizza base.

2. Put the dough onto a floured surface and roll and stretch it into a rectangle about 14 x 11 inches.

3. Grease your baking sheet with margarine and carefully lift the dough onto it. Pinch up the edge all the way around.

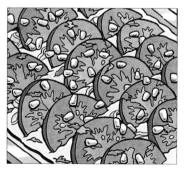

4. Peel the onion and slice it into thin rings. Crush the garlic. Gently heat the oil and cook the onion and garlic for three minutes.

5. Spread the onion rings and garlic over the dough. Cut the tomatoes in half and slice them as thinly as you can.

6. Lay the tomatoes on the base, overlapping them a little. Scatter the pine nuts and chopped basil over the top.

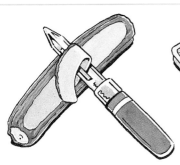

7. Trim the ends off the zucchini. Hold it in one hand and run a potato peeler along to cut really thin slices.

8. Lay the zucchini slices over the pizza. Season it with a little salt and pepper. Sprinkle on the grated cheese.

9. Put the pizza into the oven and bake for 15-20 minutes until the cheese is golden and bubbling. Serve immediately.

Calzones (folded pizzas)

Makes eight calzones

One traditional pizza base (see pages 78-79)

For the filling: 8oz. ricotta cheese
3oz. smoked Italian ham or Canadian bacon
4oz. mozzarella cheese
2 large tomatoes
salt and ground black pepper
olive oil

Heat your oven to 450°F.

1. Follow the steps on pages 78-79 to make traditional dough. While it is rising, chop up the ingredients for the filling.

2. Cut the ham into small pieces. Cut the tomatoes and shred the Mozzarella if necessary. Turn on your oven.

3. Put both types of cheese, the tomatoes, ham and a pinch of salt and pepper into a bowl. Mix them together well.

Trim the edge to make a circle if you need to.

4. When the dough has risen and you have kneaded it a second time, cut it into eight pieces. Roll the pieces into balls.

5. Sprinkle a little flour onto a work surface and roll out one of the balls to make a circle about seven inches across.

6. Put a heaping tablespoon of the mixture onto one half of the circle. Brush a little water around the edge.

7. Fold the dough over the mixture and pinch along the edges to seal the two halves. Make seven more like this.

8. Grease a baking tray with margarine. Lift the calzones onto the tray. Brush them with olive oil and put them in the oven.

9. Bake the calzones for 20-30 minutes until they have puffed up and have become golden brown.

You can eat the calzones when they are hot or cold.

Patterned edges

Instead of pinching the dough together, you can press a fork around the edge. This leaves a pattern once the calzone is cooked.

Hot apple pizza

Makes one 10-inch round pizza

For the base: 1½ cups of all purpose or bread flour
2 tablespoons butter or margarine
1 envelope of rapid rise yeast
4 tablespoons of apple juice

For the topping: 2 medium cooking apples
3 tablespoons of apple juice
1 small box of raisins
half a teaspoon of cinnamon
1 tablespoon of sugar
3 eating apples
2 tablespoons of lemon juice
1 heaped tablespoon of brown sugar

Heat your oven to 400°F.

1. Sift the flour into a bowl and add the butter or margarine. Rub the butter into the flour until it looks like breadcrumbs.

Rub in with your fingers.

2. Put the apple juice into a pan and heat it a little to make it warm. Add it and the yeast to the bowl and stir them well.

3. Continue to stir until you get a soft dough which doesn't stick to the sides of the bowl. Then squeeze it to make a ball.

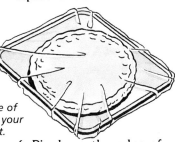

Lay the circle of dough onto your baking sheet.

4. Sprinkle flour onto a clean, dry work surface. Knead the dough until it is smooth and stretchy (see page 79).

5. Grease a pizza pan or baking sheet with margarine. Rub flour onto a rolling pin and roll the dough into a 10-inch circle.

6. Pinch up the edge of the dough to make a rim, then cover it with plastic foodwrap. Put it in a warm place for 30 minutes.

7. Peel the cooking apples and cut them in quarters. Cut out the core and then slice the rest of the apple as finely as you can.

Cut out the apple cores.

8. Put the sliced apple into a small pan. Add the apple juice and cook them with a lid on for 15 minutes until the apple is very soft.

9. Take the pan off the heat and stir the apple to make a smooth sauce, or purée. Add the raisins, sugar and cinnamon.

10. Turn the oven on. Peel the eating apples and quarter them. Slice them finely and sprinkle the slices with lemon juice.

11. Spread the purée over the dough with a spoon. Arrange the slices of apple on top, overlapping them a little.

12. Sprinkle the pizza with the brown sugar. Put it into your oven for about 15 minutes or until the dough is golden.

Pasta shapes

Each of the pasta recipes suggests a type or shape of pasta to use. However, if you don't have the right kind, here are a few suggestions for alternative types of pasta you can use. There's also a reminder of names of different types of pasta.

pages 54-55
If you don't have spaghetti, you can use linguine, vermicelli or capelli d'angelo.

page 56
Instead of using fusilli, you can use conchiglie, farfalle or penne.

page 57
If you don't have conchiglie, you can use farfalle, penne or fusilli.

pages 58-59
Use penne instead of macaroni.

page 60-61
Instead of using penne to make this dish you could use conchiglie, farfalle or fusilli.

pages 62-63
If you can't get tagliarini, you can use linguine, spaghetti or fettuccine for this recipe.

page 64
If you don't have ravioli, you can use any filled pasta, such as tortelloni or tortellini.

page 65
If you don't have tortellini, use ravioli or tortelloni, which are the same shape as tortellini, but larger.

pages 66-67
If you can't get conchiglie giganti, use cannelloni (large tubes) instead. Use a teaspoon to fill them with the spinach and ricotta mixture. Turn the cannelloni several times while they are cooking.

page 68-69
You can use fettuccine or tagliarini, instead of tagliatelle.

pages 70-71
You can use tagliatelle instead of egg noodles for this recipe.

page 72-73
You can use any tiny pasta shapes for this recipe. You can also use spaghetti, broken into small pieces. Some supermarkets sell 'soup pasta' which is a mixture of different shapes.

page 74-75
If you don't have vermicelli, you can use spaghetti or capelli d'angelo instead.

page 76-77
If you haven't farfalle, you can use conchiglie, fusilli or penne instead.

Different types of pasta

capelli d'angelo - a very thin type of spaghetti
conchiglie - shells
conchiglie giganti - very large shells.
egg noodles - very thin, flat strands, which are usually dried
farfalle - bows or 'butterflies'
fettuccine - narrow, flat strands
fusilli - spirals
linguine - flat, thin strands
macaroni - small straight or curved tubes
penne - small quill-shaped tubes cut diagonally at both ends
ravioli - square-shaped pasta, which is usually filled with meat, but is sometimes filled with cheese or vegetables.
spaghetti - long, thin, round strands
tagliarini - very thin, flat strands
tagliatelle - flat strands of pasta
tortellini - small, ring-shaped, filled pasta
vermicelli - thin, round strands, thinner than spaghetti

VEGETARIAN
COOKING
FOR BEGINNERS

Vegetarian cooking

All the recipes in this part of the book are vegetarian, which means that they contain no meat or fish. Some of the recipes are suitable for 'vegans' or 'strict vegetarians'. These recipes don't use any animal products, such as cheese or eggs. They are marked with a (v)* beside the page number in the index (see page 192).

Preparing vegetables

You should wash most fresh vegetables before you prepare them. If you are using mushrooms, don't wash them, but wipe them on a damp paper towel before slicing them. Leeks need to be washed very well to get rid of any soil which is trapped inside. Step 1 on page 122 shows you the easiest way of doing this.

Wash leeks well before you use them.

If you're not sure how to prepare garlic, turn to page 5 where there are steps which show you what to do. On page 55 you can find out how to crush a clove a garlic if you don't have a garlic crusher.

The sections at the top of broccoli or cauliflower are called florets. Cut these off the thick stalk (see page 125).

A clove of garlic is one part of a whole garlic bulb.

Use kitchen scissors to cut up fresh herbs, such as parsley or chives.

Peel carrots and potatoes if they are dirty or big. Wash or scrape new potatoes and small carrots.

Measuring with a cup or spoon

If you use a cup or spoon for measuring, make sure that the ingredient is level with the edge and not heaped up.

Getting your oven ready

Remember that all the dishes should be cooked on the middle rack of an oven, unless the recipe says something else. Always move the shelf to the right place before you turn on your oven. If you have a convection oven, read its instruction book before you start to cook. It will tell you to reduce the heat or the cooking time.

A balanced diet

Your body needs proteins, vitamins and iron to stay healthy. If you eat a vegetarian diet all the time, make sure that your food contains a good mixture of them (see page 144).

Iron can be found in things such as eggs, nuts and dried fruit.

Beans, nuts, eggs, cheese and milk all contain protein.

Cheese, milk, yogurt and eggs all contain essential vitamins. They are also found in many breakfast cereals and soya milk.

Hints and tips

This page shows you some of the cooking skills which are used in the vegetarian recipes.

Grating cheese

Cut a piece of cheese which is a little bigger than what you need, so that you do not need to grate all the way down to your fingers.

Adding salt and pepper

Try adding a pinch of salt or ground black pepper.

Some recipes tell you to add a little salt and pepper. The amount you add of each depends on your own taste.

Cutting peppers

Use a serrated knife to cut both ends off. Cut the pepper in half from end to end and cut out the part with the seeds.

If you are going to slice the pepper, it's a lot easier to cut from the inside, rather than trying to cut into the shiny skin.

Slicing tomatoes

A small serrated knife is best to use to slice a tomato. Cut the tomato in half, then lay it flat-side down and slice it.

Making breadcrumbs

1. For homemade breadcrumbs, get some two- or three-day-old bread. Cut off the crusts and tear the slices of bread into pieces.

2. Put the bread into a food processor. Put on the lid and turn it on. Whizz the bread until you get fine crumbs.

Use the small or medium holes on your grater.

If you don't have a food processor, grate stale bread on a cheese grater to make crumbs. Be careful that you don't grate your fingers.

Cheese crunchies

Makes 10-12

2oz. (¾ cup) grated mature
Cheddar cheese
½ cup soft 'tub' margarine
½ cup semolina
½ cup self-rising flour
½ cup plain whole-wheat flour
quarter of a teaspoon of salt

1. Grate the cheese on the medium holes on your grater. Put the cheese into a large bowl. Add the margarine and semolina.

2. Shake the flour and the salt through a strainer into the bowl. Add any pieces left in the bottom of the strainer.

Use a wooden spoon.

3. Stir everything well until all the ingredients are mixed together. Then, squeeze the mixture into a ball.

4. Sprinkle a clean, dry work surface with a little flour. Put the mixture onto it and shape it into a roll, about 6in. long.

5. Lay the roll on some plastic foodwrap. Wrap it around the roll. Put the roll into a refrigerator for about an hour, to chill.

The margarine greases the baking sheets.

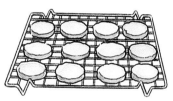

6. While the roll is in the refrigerator, dip a paper towel in some margarine, then rub it over two baking sheets.

7. Turn on your oven to 375°F. Unwrap the roll and cut it into ½in. slices. Space out the slices on the baking sheets.

8. Bake them for about 15 minutes until they are golden. When they are cooked, lift them onto a wire rack to cool.

Three-bean dip

Enough for 4-6

14oz. can of navy beans
14oz. can of pinto beans
14oz. can of cannellini beans
2 lemons
1 clove of garlic
5 tablespoons of tahini paste
4 tablespoons of boiling water
2 tablespoons of chopped parsley
salt and ground black pepper

Serve the dip with homemade breadsticks (see opposite), or with crackers.

1. Empty the beans into a strainer or colander. Rinse the beans under cold water, then drain them. Pour them into a large bowl.

Stir the beans too, to lift those at the bottom.

2. Mash the beans with a fork to make a smoothish mixture. It's quite hard work to begin with. Put some water on to boil.

3. Cut the lemons in half. Press and twist each half on a lemon squeezer. Pour the juice into the beans and mash the mixture again.

To serve, spoon the dip into a clean bowl and sprinkle on some more parsley.

4. Peel the garlic clove and crush it. Add the garlic to the beans along with the tahini, boiling water and the parsley.

5. Stir in a little salt and pepper. Then, beat the mixture with a wooden spoon until everything is mixed in thoroughly.

6. Taste it and add more salt and pepper if you need to. Put the dip into a refrigerator for at least half an hour to chill.

Breadsticks

Makes about 20

10oz. package of white bread machine mix
2 tablespoon of poppy seeds
2 tablespoons of sesame seeds
flour for work surface
margarine for greasing
yeast, if bread mix calls for it

Heat your oven to 400°F.

1. Grease two baking sheets with margarine on a paper towel. Open the bread mix and put it in a large bowl.

Find out how to knead dough on page 79.

The dough will become smooth and stretchy.

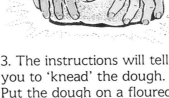

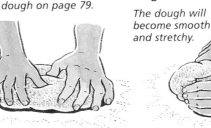

2. Add the poppy seeds and a tablespoon of sesame seeds. Begin to make the dough, following the instructions on the package.

3. The instructions will tell you to 'knead' the dough. Put the dough on a floured work surface, then push the dough away from you.

4. Fold the dough in half, turn it and push it away again. Do this for about five minutes. Leave the dough in a bowl to rise.

Cover the rest of the dough in foodwrap while you are rolling each stick.

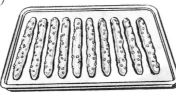

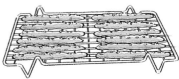

5. Turn on your oven. Cut the dough in quarters, then cut each quarter into five pieces. Roll each piece into an 8in. stick.

6. Brush each stick with cold water and sprinkle on the remaining sesame seeds. Space the sticks out on the baking sheets.

7. Cook the breadsticks for 15 minutes, until they turn golden. Use a spatula and fork to lift them onto a wire rack to cool.

Bread and cheese pudding

Enough for 4

margarine for greasing
6oz. stale white bread (about 6 slices)
4oz. Cheddar cheese
3 eggs
1¾ cups milk
½ teaspoon of spicy brown mustard

salt and ground black pepper
½ teaspoon of ground paprika
2 medium tomatoes

a shallow 1-quart ovenproof dish

Heat your oven to 400°F.

1. Dip a paper towel into some margarine. Rub the paper towel over the inside of an ovenproof dish, to grease it.

2. If the bread is unsliced, slice it. Cut the slices into squares, about 1in., leaving the crust on. Put the bread into the dish.

3. Cut the cheese into ½in. cubes, then scatter them evenly over the bread. Turn your oven on to heat up.

4. Break the eggs into a cup and beat them with a fork. Add the milk, mustard and a little salt and pepper, and whisk it.

5. Slowly pour the milky mixture over the bread and cheese. Make sure that all the pieces are coated with the mixture.

6. Leave the dish to stand for five minutes, so that the egg and milk is absorbed into the bread and it becomes slightly soggy.

7. Sprinkle small pinches of paprika over the top. Wash your hands after touching it because it will sting if you accidentally rub your eyes.

Use a serrated knife.

8. Cut the tomatoes in half and slice them as thinly as you can. Lay the slices in rows on top of the bread and cheese.

9. Put the dish into the oven and bake it for 35 minutes, until the bread is golden brown and the cheese is bubbling.

Tropical spiced rice

Enough for 4

1/3 cup shredded coconut
8oz. can of pineapple pieces in juice
1/4 teaspoon of ground tumeric
salt and ground white pepper
8oz. (1 1/3 cups) basmati and wild rice, or long-grain
  and wild rice
8 green onions
1 tablespoon of sunflower oil
1/4 teaspoon of ground coriander
1/2 cup frozen peas, thawed
1/4 cup raisins

1. Put some water on to boil. Put the shredded coconut into a measuring cup.

2. Pour 2 3/4 cups of boiling water into the cup. Stir the mixture well.

You could use long grain rice for this recipe. Follow the cooking instructions on its package.

3. Drain the pieces of pineapple through a strainer into a large cup or bowl. Don't throw away the pineapple juice.

4. Pour the coconut liquid and the pineapple juice into a large pan. Add the tumeric and half a teaspoon of salt. Bring it to a boil.

5. Put the rice into a strainer and rinse it well under cold water. Add the rice to the pan and bring it back to a boil.

Don't lift the lid while it cooks.

6. Turn the heat down so that the water is just bubbling. Put a lid on the pan. Cook the rice gently for 20 minutes.

7. While the rice is cooking, cut the top and bottom off the green onions. Slice the onions into 1in. pieces.

8. Heat the oil in a frying pan over medium heat. Add the onions and cook them for four minutes, stirring occasionally.

Stir it all the time.

Cooking rice

9. Sprinkle the coriander over the onions and cook for one minute, stirring all the time. Then, turn the heat off under this pan.

10. When the rice is cooked, add the pineapple, peas, onions, raisins and some pepper. Cook it for a minute, then eat it while it's hot.

If rice sticks together when it is cooked, separate the grains by stirring lightly with a fork.

Italian bread

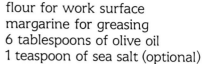

Enough for 4

2 cups all-purpose flour
1 level teaspoon of easy-blend
   dried yeast
1 cup warm water

flour for work surface
margarine for greasing
6 tablespoons of olive oil
1 teaspoon of sea salt (optional)

a baking sheet, greased with margarine

1. Shake the flour through a strainer into a large bowl. Stir in the easy-blend yeast, then make a hollow in the middle of the flour.

2. Pour the warm water into the hollow, along with five tablespoons of oil. Mix it into the flour with a wooden spoon.

3. Continue mixing the flour, oil and water until you get a soft dough which doesn't stick to the sides of the bowl.

Sprinkle about two tablespoons of flour on your work surface.

4. Sprinkle flour onto a clean, dry work surface. Dip a paper towel in margarine and grease inside a large bowl.

5. Wash your hands. 'Knead' the dough for five minutes (see page 79), then put it into the greased bowl.

6. Cover the bowl with plastic foodwrap. Leave it in a warm place for an hour, until the dough rises to twice its size.

Remember to grease the baking sheet first.

7. Then, knead the dough again for a couple of minutes, to burst all the large air bubbles which have formed inside it.

8. Sprinkle some flour onto a rolling pin, then roll out the dough to make a circle about 10in. across the middle.

9. Put the dough on a baking sheet. Rub oil onto a piece of foodwrap and cover the bread. Turn your oven on to 425°F.

Dip your finger in flour before you press it in.

10. Leave the baking sheet in a warm place (not in the oven!) for 20 minutes. Take off the foodwrap. Make dimples all over the top.

11. Brush the top with a tablespoon of oil, then sprinkle the sea salt over the top. Put the baking sheet into the oven.

12. Bake the bread for 25 minutes, until it is golden. Leave it on a wire rack to cool. Cut it into wedges, then add a filling you like.

Mexican bean soup

Enough for 4

1 small red onion
1 clove of garlic
1 tablespoon of olive oil
7oz. can of red kidney beans
1 teaspoon of mild chili powder
14½oz. can of chopped
tomatoes with herbs
1 vegetable bouillon cube

1. Peel the skin off the onion and chop the onion finely. Peel the clove of garlic and crush it. Put some water on to boil.

2. Heat the oil in a large saucepan over medium heat. Cook the onion and garlic for about five minutes until they are soft.

3. Open the can of beans, then pour them into a strainer to drain them. Rinse the beans under cold running water.

Stir until the bouillon cube dissolves.

4. Add the beans to the pan, along with the chili powder and chopped tomatoes. Stir everything together well.

5. Crumble the bouillon cube into a measuring cup. Pour in ⅔ cup of boiling water and stir well. Pour the bouillon into the pan.

6. Turn up the heat so that the mixture boils. Then, when it is boiling, turn the heat down so that the soup bubbles gently.

Softening onions

7. Put a lid on the pan and let the soup bubble for about ten minutes. Stir it occasionally to stop it from sticking.

8. Take the pan off the heat. Ladle the soup into bowls. Don't try to pour it out as it may splash. Eat it while it's hot.

When you soften onions, let them sizzle gently in oil, stirring occasionally. Turn the heat down if the onion begins to turn brown.

Bulghur wheat risotto

Enough for 4

4 green onions
4oz. button mushrooms
3 tablespoons of sunflower oil
2oz. flaked almonds
1 vegetable bouillon cube
8oz. bulghur wheat
8 ready-to-eat dried apricots
4 sprigs of fresh parsley
salt and ground black pepper

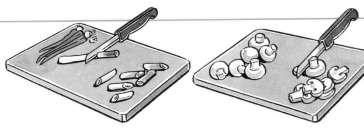

Stir the almonds all the time, as they burn easily.

1. Cut the tops and bottoms off the green onions. Cut the onions diagonally into pieces, about 1in. long.

2. Wipe the mushrooms with a damp paper towel to clean them. Then, slice each mushroom thinly. Put some water on to boil.

3. Put about half a tablespoon of oil into a saucepan, over medium heat. Cook the almonds until they are golden.

A slotted spoon has holes in it.

Stir until the cube dissolves.

4. Put a paper towel onto a plate. Use a slotted spoon to lift the almonds onto it. Then, heat the remaining oil in the pan.

5. Add the mushrooms and green onions to the pan. Cook them gently for five minutes, until they are soft. Stir them often.

6. Meanwhile, crumble the bouillon cube into a measuring cup. Pour in two cups of boiling water and stir.

Take off the lid and stir it occasionally.

7. Add the bulghur wheat to the pan and stir it for a minute. Pour in the bouillon, then turn the heat up so that the mixture boils.

8. Once it has boiled, turn the heat down and put a lid on the pan. Let the mixture bubble gently for about ten minutes.

9. Use kitchen scissors to snip the apricots into small pieces. Add the pieces to the bubbling mixture, along with some salt and pepper.

Use kitchen scissors.

10. Take the lid off the pan. Let the mixture cook for five minutes more, or until all the bouillon has been absorbed.

11. While the mixture is cooking, break the stalks off the parsley. Put the leaves into a mug and snip them into small pieces.

12. Stir the parsley and half of the flaked almonds into the mixture. Sprinkle the rest of the almonds on top and serve immediately.

Super spaghetti sauce

Enough for 4

1 onion
1 stick of celery
4oz. button mushrooms
2 medium carrots
1 clove of garlic
3 tablespoons of olive oil
1 vegetable bouillon cube

14oz. can of chopped tomatoes
1 tablespoon of Italian seasoning
4oz. meatless burger mix
salt and ground black pepper
12oz. dried pasta or 15oz. fresh pasta
1 tablespoon margarine

1. Cut the ends off the onion and celery. Peel the onion and wash the celery. Cut both the onion and celery into thin slices.

2. Wipe the mushrooms with a damp paper towel. Cut them into thick slices. Peel or scrape the carrots, then slice them finely.

3. Peel and crush the garlic. Heat two tablespoons of oil in a large pan over a low heat. Add the onion and cook it for three minutes.

4. Add the celery, carrots, mushrooms and garlic. Cook them for five minutes, until the onion begins to turn brown.

5. While the vegetables are cooking, put some water on to boil. Crumble the bouillon cube into a measuring cup.

6. Pour two cups of boiling water into the measuring cup and stir until the bouillon cube dissolves.

Stir it occasionally to stop it from sticking.

7. Pour the bouillon into the pan. Add the chopped tomatoes, Italian seasoning and a little salt and pepper. Stir the mixture well.

8. Stir in the burger mix. Turn up the heat and bring the mixture to a boil. Then, turn down the heat so that it bubbles gently.

9. Put a lid on the pan and cook the mixture for 30 minutes. The mixture will thicken as the burger soaks up the bouillon.

The oil will stop the pasta from sticking.

Drain the pasta in a colander.

10. About 15 minutes before the sauce is ready, half-fill a large pan with water. Add a tablespoon of oil and a pinch of salt.

11. Bring the water to a boil and add the pasta. Look at the instructions on the package of pasta and cook it for the time it says.

12. When the pasta is cooked, drain it, then put it back into the pan. Add the margarine and shake the pan to coat the pasta.

13. Put the pasta onto four plates or bowls. Ladle some sauce on top and eat it immediately.

Cheese and tomato tart

Enough for 4-6

13oz. package of ready-rolled puff pastry
1 tablespoon of milk
1 large onion
1 medium zucchini
3 tablespoons of olive oil
half a teaspoon of dried oregano
salt and ground black pepper
8oz. cherry tomatoes
8oz. mozzarella cheese

Trim the pastry to fit the tray.

1. Turn your oven on to 425°F. Unroll the pastry. Put it on a baking sheet. Trim one end off, if you need to.

2. Put the milk into a cup. Use a pastry brush to brush the milk around the edge of the pastry, to make a ½ in. border.

3. Cut the ends off the onion and peel it. Cut it finely. Cut the ends off the zucchini and cut it into ½ in. slices.

The onion and zucchini will soften.

4. Heat the oil over lowish heat and add the onion. Cook it for five minutes. Add the zucchini and cook for five minutes more.

5. Stir in the oregano and add some salt and pepper. Spoon the mixture over the pastry, but do not cover the milky border.

6. Use a serrated knife to cut the tomatoes in half. Arrange the tomatoes on top of the mixture, with their cut-side upward.

This tart is delicious served hot or warm.

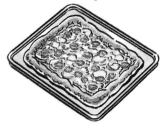

7. Open the bag of cheese and pour away any liquid. Cut the cheese into ½ in. cubes. Scatter them evenly over the tomatoes.

8. Put the tart on the middle rack of the oven for 35-40 minutes, until the pastry rises around the edges and turns brown.

9. Leave the tart on the baking sheet for three minutes. Cut the tart into eight pieces. Use a spatula to lift each piece.

Veggie burgers

Makes 8

1 onion
1 stick of celery
1 red pepper
2 tablespoons of sunflower oil
1 clove of garlic
6oz. dried red lentils
1 vegetable bouillon cube
half a teaspoon of yeast extract
3oz. fresh breadcrumbs (approx. 3 slices)
2oz. chopped nuts
ground black pepper

Stir it occasionally.

1. Cut the ends off the onion and celery. Peel the onion and wash the celery. Cut them both into very thin pieces.

2. Slice the ends off the red pepper. Cut it in half and cut out the seeds. Cut each half into thin strips. Cut the strips into cubes.

3. Put some water on to boil. Heat the oil in a pan over medium heat. Cook the onion and celery for five minutes, until soft.

Stir it all the time, to coat everything with oil.

4. Peel and crush the garlic. Add it to the pan, along with the red pepper and lentils. Cook them for about a minute.

5. Crumble the bouillon cube into a measuring cup and pour in 1½ cups of boiling water. Add the yeast extract and stir well.

6. Pour the bouillon into the pan and bring it to a boil. Then, turn the heat down until the mixture bubbles gently. Put a lid on the pan.

Cover it with plastic foodwrap.

7. Cook the mixture for 25 minutes, or until the lentils have absorbed all the bouillon. Spoon the mixture into a large bowl.

8. Mix in the breadcrumbs, nuts and some pepper. Let the mixture cool, then cover it. Put it in a refrigerator for at least 30 minutes.

9. When chilled, divide the mixture into eight pieces. Sprinkle some flour on a chopping board and roll each piece into a ball.

Use a spatula to turn the burgers over.

10. Turn your broiler on to medium. Press each ball into a burger shape and brush the top of each one with a little oil.

11. Put the burgers onto the broiler-pan rack. Cook them under the broiler for five minutes, until they are slightly browned.

12. Turn the burgers over. Brush the tops with a little more oil and cook them for five more minutes. Eat them while they are hot.

Mushroom croustade

Enough for 4

For the case:
½ cup whole-wheat flour
¼ cup oatmeal
1 cup breadcrumbs (find out how to make breadcrumbs on page 100)
½ cup butter or margarine

For the filling:
8oz. button mushrooms
1 tablespoon of sunflower oil
2 eggs
5oz. vegetarian cream-style cheese with herbs and garlic
salt and ground black pepper

an 8 inch quiche dish

Mix them with a wooden spoon.

1. Turn your oven on to 400°F. to heat up. For the case, put the flour, oatmeal and breadcrumbs into a large bowl.

2. Gently melt the butter or margarine in a pan over low heat. Pour in the mixture from the bowl and mix it well.

3. Spoon the mixture into a quiche dish. Use the back of a spoon to press it firmly onto the bottom and up the sides of the dish.

The baking sheet helps the mixture to cook on the bottom.

4. Put the dish onto a baking sheet. Bake it on the middle shelf of your oven for ten minutes. Take it out of the oven.

5. Turn the oven down to 350°F. Wipe the mushrooms using a damp paper towel, then cut them in half.

Stir the mushrooms occasionally.

6. Heat the oil in a frying pan over low heat. Add the mushrooms and cook them for five minutes, until they are soft.

Put the bowl on a damp cloth to stop it from slipping.

7. Turn the heat off under the mushrooms. Break the eggs into a small bowl and beat them with a fork until they are mixed.

Use a wooden spoon.

8. Put the cheese into a bowl and stir it. Add the beaten egg, a little at a time. Stir the mixture each time you add some egg.

9. Add the mushrooms to the mixture, but don't add any of the juice left in the pan. Add some salt and pepper and stir well.

*The croustade
is delicious served
with a salad or
green vegetables.*

10. Spoon the mixture into the case and smooth the top with the back of a spoon. Press in any mushrooms sticking up.

11. Put the dish into the oven for 25 minutes and bake it until the filling has set and the crust is golden. Serve it hot or cold.

Cheesy sausages

Makes 8

1 small leek
1 tablespoon butter
4oz. Cheddar cheese
8 fresh chives
2 eggs
salt and ground black pepper
¼ teaspoon of mustard powder
1½ cups (6oz.) white breadcrumbs
2 tablespoons of all-purpose flour
2 tablespoons of sunflower oil

Slice halfway along the leek from the green end, like this.

Use a small saucepan.

Snip the chives over the bowl.

1. Cut the roots and green tops off the leek. Make a slice halfway along the leek and rinse it really well to get rid of any soil. Then, slice the leek finely.

2. Melt the butter in a saucepan over medium heat. Add the slices of leek and cook gently for about five minutes, until soft. Don't let them go brown.

3. Spoon the leek into a big bowl. Grate the cheese finely and add it to the bowl. Use kitchen scissors to snip the chives into small pieces and add them too.

Put a damp dishcloth under the bowl to stop it from slipping as you beat.

Find out how to make breadcrumbs on page 100.

4. Break the eggs into a small bowl. Add some salt and pepper and the mustard. Beat them lightly until the yolks, egg white and mustard are mixed.

5. Pour the beaten egg mixture into the big bowl and add the breadcrumbs. Stir everything together with a wooden spoon until it is mixed well.

6. Sprinkle a little flour onto a clean, dry work surface. Put the mixture onto the flour and cut it into eight equal pieces with a knife.

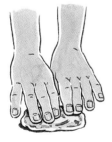

Turn the sausages often as they cook.

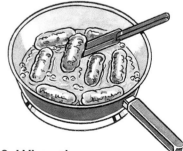

7. Wash your hands and dry them. Rub a little flour on your hands, then roll each piece into the shape of a sausage. Put the sausages onto a plate.

8. Cover the sausages with some plastic foodwrap. Put the plate into a refrigerator for about 20 minutes, to make the sausages firm.

9. When the sausages are ready, heat the oil in a frying pan over medium heat. Add the sausages and cook them for ten minutes. Serve immediately.

Chunky vegetable goulash

Enough for 4

1 onion
1 clove of garlic
2 carrots
2 medium-sized potatoes

half a head of cauliflower
1 tablespoon of vegetable oil
3 teaspoons of paprika
1 tablespoon of flour
1 vegetable bouillon cube
14½ oz. can of chopped tomatoes
    with herbs
        salt and ground black pepper
            ⅔ cup sour cream

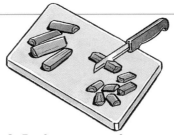

1. Cut the top and bottom off the onion. Peel the onion and cut it into small chunks. Peel the clove of garlic and crush it.

2. Peel or scrape the carrots and cut them in half. Cut them lengthwise, then slice them into pieces about an inch long.

3. Peel the potatoes and cut them in half. Cut each piece of potato into ½in. slices, then cut the slices into cubes.

4. Pull any leaves off the cauliflower and throw them away. Cut the florets off the cauliflower's stalk (see tip below).

5. Heat the oil in a large pan over lowish heat. Gently cook the onion and garlic for five minutes, until they are soft.

6. While the onions are cooking, put some water on to boil. Sprinkle 2 teaspoons of paprika over the onions. Add the flour and stir well.

7. Crumble the bouillon cube into a measuring cup and pour in 2¾ cups of boiling water. Stir it until the cube dissolves.

8. Pour the bouillon into the pan. Add the tomatoes, carrots, potatoes and the cauliflower florets, as well as a little salt and pepper.

9. Turn the heat up and bring the mixture to a boil. Then, turn down the heat so that the mixture bubbles gently.

Cutting cauliflower

10. Put a lid on the pan. Leave everything to bubble gently for about 20-25 minutes, until the vegetables are cooked.

11. Use a ladle to put the goulash into bowls. Spoon on some sour cream and sprinkle the remaining paprika on top.

Cut into the stalk about ½in. from a floret. Pull the floret out, then cut off another one.

Baked Spanish omelette

Enough for 4

margarine for greasing
1 onion
2 medium potatoes
2 tablespoons of olive oil
1 clove of garlic
¾ cup frozen peas, thawed
4 eggs
⅔ cup milk
salt and ground black pepper

a shallow 8-inch ovenproof dish

1. Turn your oven on to 350°F. Dip a paper towel in some margarine, then rub it over the inside of the dish.

2. Peel the onion and cut it finely. Peel the potatoes and cut them in half. Cut them into ½ in. slices. Cut the slices into cubes.

Stir it occasionally.

3. Heat the oil in a frying pan over medium heat. Add the onion and potato and cook for four minutes, until they begin to soften.

Stir it all the time.

4. Peel and crush the garlic. Add it to the pan and cook for two minutes more, until the onion and potatoes begin to brown.

5. Take the pan off the heat. Spoon the onion and potato into the bottom of the dish spreading it out evenly. Add the peas too.

6. Break the eggs into a small bowl. Beat them with a fork, then stir in the milk and a little salt and black pepper.

7. Pour the beaten egg over the vegetables in the dish. Bake the omelette in the oven for 45 minutes until it has set.

8. To check that it is cooked, push a knife into the middle of it. If lots of liquid seeps out, cook it for a few more minutes.

9. Run a knife around the edge of the dish to loosen the omelette, then cut it into quarters. Use a spatula to serve it.

Other fillings : Cheese

Sprinkle 2oz. of grated Swiss cheese and one tablespoon of chopped parsley over the vegetables, at step 5.

Mushroom

For a mushroom omelette, leave out the peas. Slice 4oz. of mushrooms. Cook them with the onions and potatoes at step 3.

Tomato

Slice two medium-sized tomatoes as finely as you can. Arrange the slices on top of the cooked vegetables, at step 5.

Corn

Drain a 7oz. can of corn in a strainer or colander. Sprinkle the corn over the vegetables at step 5.

Cheese bites with tomato sauce

Enough for 4

For the tomato sauce:
1 red onion
1 tablespoon of olive oil
14oz. can of chopped tomatoes
2 tablespoons of soy sauce
2 teaspoons of red wine vinegar
1 teaspoon of soft brown sugar

For the cheese bites:
3oz. (¾ cup) white breadcrumbs
2 tablespoons of plain flour
8oz. Cheddar cheese
salt and ground black pepper
2 eggs (you only need the whites)
oil for frying

Grate the cheese on the medium holes on your grater.

1. Make the breadcrumbs (see page 4). Put ½ cup (2oz.) of the breadcrumbs into a bowl. Grate the cheese, add it and stir well.

Slice the onion as thinly as you can.

2. Put the bowl on one side while you make the sauce. Cut the ends off the onion and peel it. Cut it in half, then slice it.

3. Put the olive oil into a pan over a low heat. Cook the slices of onion for five minutes, stirring them occasionally.

4. Add the tomatoes, soy sauce, vinegar and sugar and stir it well. Turn up the heat and bring the mixture to a boil.

5. Once the mixture has boiled, turn down the heat and let it bubble gently. Put a lid on the pan and cook for 15 minutes.

6. Make the bites while the sauce is cooking. Shake the flour and some salt and pepper through a strainer onto the cheese.

Make sure that the bowl is clean before you start.

7. Carefully break one egg onto a saucer. Put an egg cup over the yolk. Tip the saucer over a bowl so that the white dribbles into it.

You don't need the yolks.

8. Do the same with the other egg. Whisk the egg white until it is stiff and makes points or 'peaks' when you lift your whisk.

9. If the tomato sauce is ready while you are still cooking the bites, turn down the heat under it, as low as it will go.

10. Stir a large spoonful of the egg white into the cheese and breadcrumb mixture. Then, gently stir in the rest of the white.

11. Wash your hands. Put the remaining breadcrumbs onto a plate. Make 16 balls with the mixture, about the size of ping pong balls.

12. Roll the balls in the crumbs to coat them. Pour about ½in. of oil into a frying pan. Turn the heat on to medium.

Use a spatula to lift them into the pan.

13. After a minute or so, put eight balls into the pan. Cook them for five minutes. Turn the balls as they cook so they are golden all over.

14. Use a slotted spoon to lift them out. Put them onto some paper towels to drain. Cook the rest of the balls in the same way.

15. Put four balls onto each plate. Stir the tomato sauce, then spoon it over the balls. Eat them while they are hot.

You could put some sauce onto each plate before you add the bites. Spoon any remaining sauce on top.

Tofu skewers with noodles

Enough for 4

20oz. package of firm tofu
2 tablespoons of soy sauce
1 small onion
1 clove of garlic
2 tablespoons of sunflower oil
¼ cup shredded coconut
1 tablespoon of lemon or lime juice

1 tablespoon of soft brown sugar
¼ teaspoon of chili powder
2 tablespoons of crunchy peanut butter

For the noodles:
1 tablespoon of oil
8oz. dried or 12oz. fresh egg noodles
1 vegetable bouillon cube
2 tablespoons of chopped parsley
  or coriander

eight skewers or kebab sticks
    (If you use wooden sticks, soak
        them in water for ten minutes
          before you begin.)

Use medium heat.

1. Open the package of tofu and drain off any liquid. Pat the tofu dry on a paper towel, then cut it into one inch cubes.

2. Push the cubes onto the sticks. Put a tablespoon of soy sauce into a bowl and brush it all over the cubes. Put some water on to boil.

3. Peel the onion and cut it finely. Peel and crush the garlic. Heat the oil in a saucepan and cook the onion and garlic until soft.

Stir until the coconut dissolves.

4. Put the shredded coconut in a bowl. Pour in three tablespoons of boiling water and stir.

5. Add the lemon or lime juice, the brown sugar, chili powder, peanut butter and a tablespoon of soy sauce.

6. Stir everything together until it is blended, then mix in the onion and garlic. Brush the mixture over the tofu.

The oil stops the noodles from sticking together.

Watch the tofu, it can burn easily.

7. Half-fill a large saucepan with water and bring it to a boil. Crumble the bouillon cube and stir it in. Add a tablespoon of oil.

8. Turn the broiler on to medium. Put the tofu sticks onto the rack in the broiler pan and put the pan under the broiler.

9. Cook the tofu for eight minutes in total. Every two minutes, turn the sticks and brush the tofu with more peanut mixture.

Time the cooking from when the noodles began to boil.

10. Meanwhile, add the noodles to the water. Let the water boil again, then turn down the heat so the water bubbles gently.

11. Cook the noodles for the time it says on their package then drain them. Put them back into the pan. Add the parsley or coriander.

12. Toss the noodles in the parsley or coriander. Put the noodles onto plates and lay two tofu sticks on top. Eat while hot.

Eggs flamenco

Enough for 4

1 medium onion
1 small red pepper
1 small yellow pepper
1 clove of garlic
1 zucchini
2 tablespoons of olive oil

14½ oz. can of chopped tomatoes
1 teaspoon of bouquet garni
salt and ground black pepper
butter or margarine for greasing
4 eggs

a shallow, ovenproof dish

1. Turn on your oven to 375°F. Cut the ends off the onion and peel it. Slice the onion as finely as you can.

2. Slice the ends off the peppers and cut them in half. Cut out the seeds. Cut the peppers into strips, then into cubes.

3. Peel the clove of garlic and crush it in a garlic press. Cut the ends off the zucchini and cut it into thin slices.

Stir the mixture occasionally.

4. Heat the oil in a pan over medium heat. Add the onions, garlic, peppers and zucchini. Cook them for ten minutes.

5. When the vegetables are soft, add the tomatoes, herbs and a pinch of salt and pepper. Stir it and let the mixture bubble.

6. Leave the mixture to cook for about five minutes, or until the sauce becomes thicker and the amount has reduced a little.

Space the hollows evenly.

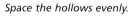

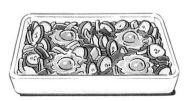

7. While the mixture is cooking, dip a paper towel into some margarine or butter. Rub it over an ovenproof dish to grease it.

8. When the mixture is ready, spoon it into the dish. Use the back of the spoon to make four hollows in the mixture.

9. Carefully crack an egg into each hollow. Lift the dish into the oven, without letting the eggs spill out over the mixture.

Breaking eggs

Bake the mixture until the egg whites have set.

10. Cook the eggs for about 10-15 minutes if you like runny yolks, or 15-20 minutes if you like your eggs well-cooked.

To break an egg, tap it sharply on the side of a bowl or a cup. Tap it again, but harder, if the shell doesn't crack the first time.

Push your thumbs inside the crack and pull the shell apart gently. Try not to let any pieces of shell fall into the bowl or cup.

Vegetarian sausages in batter

Enough for 4

12oz. package of vegetarian sausages,
   thawed if frozen
1 medium zucchini
6 cherry tomatoes
½ cup flour

¼ teaspoon of salt
¼ cup milk
1 egg
2 tablespoons solid white vegetable
   shortening

a 8-inch round pan

Use a large bowl.

1. Turn your oven on to 425°F. to heat up. Cut each sausage into three equal-sized pieces.

2. Cut the ends off the zucchini. Cut it into one inch slices. Prick the skin of each tomato with the tip of a sharp knife.

3. To make the batter, shake the flour and salt through a strainer. Then, make a hollow in the middle of the flour.

4. Pour the milk into a measuring cup and add ¼ cup of cold water to make ½ cup of liquid altogether.

5. Break the egg into a cup, then pour it into the hollow in the flour. Pour in half of the milky liquid from the cup, too.

Whisk it until you get a smooth batter.

6. Mix the milky liquid with the flour. Add the rest of the liquid, a little at a time. Whisk it well each time you add some.

7. Put the fat into the pan and put it in the oven for five minutes. Then, wearing oven mitts, very carefully lift the pan out.

8. Spread the sausages and vegetables around the pan. Be careful, the fat will be hot. Then, pour the batter over them.

9. Bake it on the top rack of the oven for 30-35 minutes, until it has risen and has turned golden. Cut into four and serve.

Tortillas with black bean filling

Enough for 4

margarine or oil for greasing
1 small onion
1 clove of garlic
1 tablespoon of olive oil
two 14½oz. cans of black beans or
   pinto beans
two 14½oz. cans of chopped tomatoes
   with basil
1 tablespoon of tomato purée

2 tablespoons of dried cilantro
1 tablespoon of mild chili powder
salt and ground black pepper
10oz. Cheddar cheese
8 ready-made flour tortillas
½ cup sour cream or plain yogurt

a large shallow, ovenproof dish, about
   14 x 8in.

Heat your oven 400°F.

1. Dip a paper towel into some margarine or pour a little oil onto it. Rub the paper towel inside the dish, to grease it.

2. Turn your oven on. Cut the ends off the onion and peel it, then slice it finely. Peel the clove of garlic and crush it.

3. Heat the oil in a saucepan. Cook the onion and the garlic over medium heat for five minutes, until soft.

Drain the beans in a strainer or a colander.

4. Drain the beans. Rinse them under cold running water. Add them to the pan and cook for a minute, stirring all the time.

5. Stir in the chopped tomatoes, tomato purée, cilantro and chili powder. Add a little salt and pepper, too.

6. Turn up the heat and bring the sauce to a boil. Then, turn the heat down so that the sauce is still bubbling, but more gently.

The sauce should be thick enough to sit on the spoon.

7. Let the sauce cook for 20 minutes, stirring now and then to stop it from sticking. The sauce should begin to thicken.

8. If your sauce doesn't start to thicken, turn the heat up a little until the mixture bubbles more. Stir it often.

9. While the sauce is cooking, grate the cheese on the large holes on the grater. Lay the tortillas on a clean, dry work surface.

*Be careful as you roll them.
The sauce is still hot.*

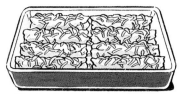

10. Divide the sauce between the tortillas. Spread it out almost to the edges, with the back of a spoon.

11. Sprinkle half of the cheese over the tortillas, then roll them up. Then, lay them, seam-side down, in the dish.

12. Sprinkle the rest of the cheese over the tortillas. Bake them for 15 minutes, then serve them with the sour cream or yogurt.

Stuffed peppers

Enough for 4

4 medium peppers
4 tablespoons of olive oil
1 vegetable bouillon cube
6oz. (1 cup) long-grain rice
1 small red onion
1 clove of garlic
7oz. can of chopped tomatoes
half a teaspoon of dried bouquet garni
½ cup frozen peas, thawed
salt and ground black pepper

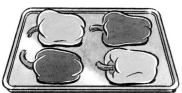

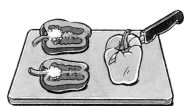

1. Turn your oven on to 400°F. Wash and dry the peppers, then put them onto a baking sheet.

2. Put two tablespoons of oil in a cup. Brush it over the peppers. Put the sheet into the oven and bake the peppers for 12 minutes.

3. When the peppers are cooked, leave them until they are cool enough to touch. Cut them in half from top to bottom.

Pour the bouillon into a large pan.

4. Cut the stalk, core and seeds from each pepper. Pat the peppers dry, then put them back onto the sheet. Put some water on to boil.

5. Crumble the bouillon cube into a cup. Pour 2¾ cups of boiling water into the cup. Stir well and pour the bouillon into a pan.

6. Add another 2¾ cups of boiling water. Pour in the rice and stir well. Turn the heat down so the mixture bubbles gently.

7. Leave the rice to cook for about ten minutes until it is just tender, then drain it in a large strainer over a sink.

8. While the rice is cooking, cut the ends off the onion and peel it. Slice the onion as finely as you can. Peel and crush the garlic.

9. Heat two tablespoons of oil in a pan. Add the onion and garlic, and cook them gently until they are soft.

The oil stops the foil from sticking to the peppers.

10. Stir in the tomatoes, herbs and a little salt and pepper. Leave the mixture to bubble gently for about five minutes.

11. Add the rice and peas to the tomato mixture and mix everything well. Spoon the mixture into the halves of pepper.

12. Spread a little oil onto the dull side of a piece of foil. Cover the peppers. Put them into the oven for ten minutes. Eat while hot.

Spinach strudel

Enough for 4

4oz. pine nuts
6oz. frozen chopped spinach, thawed
9oz. ricotta cheese
quarter of a teaspoon of grated nutmeg
salt and ground black pepper

3 tablespoons butter
4oz. fillo dough (about 8 sheets)
1 tablespoon of poppy seeds
1 tablespoon Italian seasoning

Heat your oven to 400°F.

1. Turn on your oven. Put the pine nuts on a baking sheet. Bake them in the oven for five minutes, until golden. Let them cool.

2. Put the spinach into a strainer. Press the spinach with the back of a large spoon, to squeeze out as much liquid as you can.

3. Put the spinach into a bowl. Mix in the pine nuts, the ricotta cheese, nutmeg, Italian seasoning and a little salt and pepper.

Cover the rest of the dough, (see tip, below right).

Don't forget to brush each sheet with butter before putting another one on top.

4. Put the butter into a small saucepan. Heat it very gently over a low heat until the butter melts. Don't let it burn.

5. Carefully lift one sheet of fillo dough and put it on a clean dish towel. Brush the sheet of dough with some of the melted butter.

6. Put another sheet of fillo dough on top and brush it with butter. Add the other sheets of dough, one by one, in the same way.

Spread out the mixture with a spatula.

Roll it like a Swiss roll.

7. Spoon the spinach mixture onto the dough. Spread it over the dough, leaving a one inch border around the edge.

8. Fold each of the short sides of dough over carefully, so that they overlap the edge of the spinach mixture.

9. Fold one of the long sides of dough over onto the mixture. Then, roll it over and over until you reach the other long side.

10. Brush some of the melted butter over a baking sheet to grease it. Lift the strudel onto it, seam-side down.

11. Brush the top and sides of the strudel with the rest of the melted butter. Sprinkle poppy seeds all over the top.

12. Bake the strudel in the oven for 20 minutes, until it is golden and crisp. Cut it into slices and eat it right away.

Using fillo dough

To stop fillo dough from drying out, cover the sheets of dough with a clean, damp dish towel until you need to use them.

Nut crumble

Enough for 4

1 carrot and 1 parsnip
8oz. broccoli
8oz. turnips
8oz. sweet potato
salt and ground black pepper
1 onion
3 tablespoons butter
⅓ cup plain flour
2 cups milk

1 teaspoon dried bouquet garni
margarine for greasing

For the crumble:
1 cup flour
⅓ cup butter
⅓ cup oatmeal
2oz. chopped mixed nuts

a large ovenproof dish

1. Turn your oven on to 375°F. Peel the carrot and the parsnip. Cut them into 1in. pieces.

2. Cut the florets off the broccoli stalks. Peel the turnip and sweet potato and cut them in half. Cut each half into 1in. slices.

3. Cut the slices of turnip and sweet potato into cubes. Half-fill a large saucepan with water and add half a teaspoon of salt.

4. Bring the pan of water to a boil. Add the carrot, parsnip, turnip and sweet potato and bring the water back to a boil.

5. Turn down the heat so that the water bubbles gently, then put a lid on the pan. Leave it to cook for five minutes.

6. Add the broccoli and cook it for five minutes more. Ladle ⅔ cup of the cooking water into a cup. Drain away the rest.

Stir the onion occasionally.

7. To make the sauce, cut the ends off the onion, peel it and slice it. Melt the butter over low heat. Cook the onion for five minutes.

8. Stir in the flour and cook it for one minute. Take the pan off the heat and add a little of the milk. Stir it really well.

9. Continue stirring in the milk, a little at a time. Stir in the water you saved from cooking the vegetables and the bouquet garni.

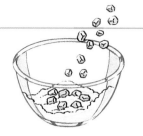

10. Put the pan back onto the heat. Bring the sauce to a boil slowly, stirring all the time. Let the sauce boil for one minute.

11. Grease the dish with margarine. Spoon in the vegetables and sprinkle on some pepper. Pour the sauce over the vegetables.

12. To make the crumble, shake the flour through a strainer into a large bowl. Cut the butter into small chunks. Add it to the bowl.

13. Rub the butter into the flour with your fingertips. Lift it up and let it fall as you do it. Continue until it looks like breadcrumbs.

14. Stir in the oatmeal and nuts. Use a spoon to sprinkle the crumble evenly over the vegetables to cover them.

15. Bake the crumble in the oven for 35 minutes. The topping will turn golden brown. Spoon it onto plates and eat while it's hot.

Healthy eating

It's important that you eat a well-balanced diet. This means that you should eat a mixture of things like bread, milk, cheese, eggs, peas, beans and lentils, as well as lots of fruit and vegetables. Try to eat food from the following groups each day. All the food you eat contains substances called nutrients, which keep your body healthy. These are proteins, carbohydrates, fats, vitamins and minerals. You also need fiber and water.

Food	Nutrients
Group 1 : soya milk or cow's milk, cheese, eggs or soya products, such as tofu and soya mince.	protein and minerals, especially calcium
Group 2 : pulses, such as, kidney beans, baked beans, chick peas, lentils; nuts such as almonds, walnuts, hazelnuts, sesame seeds, sunflower seeds.	protein, carbohydrates, fiber, vitamins and minerals
Group 3 : vegetable oil, margarine, butter.	vitamins, fat
Group 4 : bread, pasta, rice, potatoes, wheat products, including flour.	carbohydrates, fiber, vitamins and minerals
Group 5: Fruit and vegetables, including dried fruit, frozen and canned vegetables.	vitamin C, fiber and minerals
Group 6 : eggs, cheese, yeast extract, fortified soya milk, fortified breakfast cereals.	vitamin B. You should eat a little of one of these each day, especially if you eat a vegan diet (see page 98).

A well-balanced meal

Most of the dishes in this book are made up of different types of nutrients, making them well-balanced meals. They contain types of food from the different groups above.

For example, the 'Tortillas with black bean sauce', on page 136, contain beans from group 2, cheese from groups 1 and 6, and tomatoes from group 5. The tortillas are made from flour which is in group 4. However, the dish doesn't contain many fresh vegetables, so it would be a good idea to serve the tortillas with a salad and to eat some fruit afterwards.

Here are a few suggestions for making other dishes in the book well-balanced:-

page 6 - serve the tomato and mozzarella salad with bread, such as the Italian bread on pages 108-109. Eat some dried raisins or apricots afterwards.

pages 122-123 - serve the cheesy sausages with some green vegetables, such as broccoli, green beans, peas or a green salad.

pages 134-135 - serve the vegetarian sausages with baked beans.

CAKES
& COOKIES
FOR BEGINNERS

Before you bake

Before you start to bake, read the tips on these two pages. Don't forget to check that you have all the ingredients and equipment you will need, before you begin.

In most types of cooking, it doesn't matter if you change an ingredient or leave something out, but you can't do this when you are baking. It's also important that you measure things exactly and use the right size of pan, otherwise your cakes or cookies may not turn out correctly.

Take butter or margarine out of the refrigerator at least 30 minutes before you use it, unless the recipe says something different.

Always use large-sized eggs unless the recipe says something else.

When you measure with a spoon, use a level spoonful, not a heaped one.

Equipment

If you are making a cake, use the size and shape of pan written in the recipe. If you use a different size, you may not have the correct amount of mixture.

Cookie sheets

All the cookies are baked on cookie sheets. Space out the uncooked cookies as they usually increase in size as they cook. When you use two cookie sheets, put them into your oven one above the other. Cook the top one for the time the recipe says, then take it out. Move the bottom one up and cook until it's ready.

Your oven

Turn your oven on when the recipe tells you to, so that it heats up.

Preparing cake pans

You need to grease a cake pan or cookie sheet to stop the cake or cookie mixture from sticking to it when it's cooked. To grease a pan, dip a paper towel into soft butter or margarine. Rub the towel over the inside. In some recipes you also need to line the pan with wax paper or rice paper, or sprinkle it with flour. To flour a pan after you have greased it, add a tablespoon or two of flour.

Cooling

Make sure that you always wear oven mitts when you take anything out of the oven. Leave cakes or cookies in their pan or on the cookie sheets for several minutes to cool. Then, put them on a wire rack to cool down completely.

Grease the sides too.

Tip the pan from side to side, until there is a light dusting all over. Throw away the excess flour.

Which rack?

Cook your cake or cookies on a rack in the middle of your oven unless the recipe says something different. Always move the rack to the middle before you turn on your oven. Don't leave an empty rack above it.

To remove a cake from a loose-bottomed cake pan, put the pan onto a can. Press on the side of the pan so that it slides down.

To turn a cake out of a cake pan, put a wire rack on top of the pan. Turn it over so that the cake comes out.

Baking tips

These pages give you lots of cooking hints and tips that will help you bake successfully. You'll also find other hints with some of the recipes.

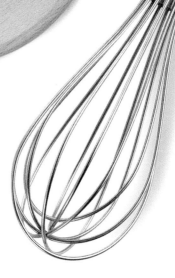

Breaking an egg

1. Crack the egg sharply on the rim of a cup or bowl. Push your thumbs into the crack in the shell and pull the sides apart.

2. Before you add an egg to a mixture, break the egg into a separate cup or bowl. It helps you to pick out any shell which may fall in.

Separating eggs

Don't let the yolk break.

Leave the yolk on the saucer.

Egg whites will not whisk if the bowl or whisk are greasy.

1. You will need a bowl and a saucer for this. Crack the egg on the side of the bowl, then pour it slowly onto the saucer.

2. Carefully put a small cup over the yolk. Tip the saucer over the bowl so that the egg white dribbles into it.

If you are whisking the egg whites, make sure that your bowl and whisk are clean and dry before you start (see page 173).

Beating eggs

Beat with the fork like this.

Beating a cake mixture

If you are beating eggs, you can use a fork instead of a whisk. Beat them until the white and yolk are mixed together.

1. Before you begin to beat, put your bowl on a damp dishcloth. This stops the bowl from slipping as you beat.

2. Stir the mixture briskly with a wooden spoon or a whisk. You are trying to get the mixture as smooth and creamy as you can.

Sifting

Shake the strainer until all the flour falls through.

Put a strainer over a bowl and pour the flour into it. If you sift whole-wheat flour, tip any bran left in the strainer into the bowl.

Rubbing in

Do this with clean, dry hands.

1. Cut the butter or margarine into small pieces and stir it into the flour. Stir until each piece is covered with flour.

2. Rub the pieces with your fingertips. Lift the mixture and let it fall as you rub. Do this until it becomes like fine breadcrumbs.

Rolling out dough

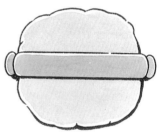

Shape the dough with your hands to keep it circular.

1. Sprinkle a clean, dry work surface with a little flour. Put the dough onto it, then sprinkle a rolling pin with some flour.

2. Press the rolling pin onto the dough and roll it away from you. Turn the dough in a quarter turn and roll it again.

3. Continue rolling and turning to make a circle, until you get the thickness of dough written in the recipe.

Melting chocolate

Stir the chocolate as it melts.

Testing a cake

1. Heat about an inch of water in a pan so that it is bubbling gently. Break the chocolate into a heatproof bowl.

2. Put on some oven mitts and lift the bowl into the pan. The heat from the water melts the chocolate gradually.

At the end of the cooking time, test your cake to see if it is cooked. Press it in the middle. If it is cooked, it will feel firm and spring up.

Peanut butter cookies

Makes 12 cookies

4 tablespoons butter or margarine
¾ cup packed soft light brown sugar
½ cup crunchy peanut butter
½ cup self-rising flour
1 cup oatmeal
1 large egg

For the topping:
  ½ cup chopped peanuts

1. Grease two cookie sheets with butter or margarine. Turn the oven on to 325°F so that it can heat up.

2. Put the margarine or butter into a large bowl. Add the sugar and peanut butter. Beat them until they are light and creamy.

3. Put a strainer over the bowl and sift the flour onto the mixture. Add the oatmeal and stir well to mix everything together.

4. Press the mixture with your fingers, then fold it in half and press again. Do this again and again until it makes a soft dough.

5. Divide the mixture in half, then in quarters until you make 12 pieces. Squeeze each piece to make a small ball.

6. Put the balls onto the cookie sheets, leaving plenty of space between them. Flatten them slightly with your hand.

7. Break the egg into a small bowl and beat it well with a fork. Brush the top of each cookie with some beaten egg.

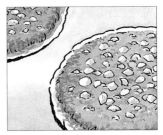

8. Sprinkle the chopped peanuts all over the top of each cookie. They will stick to the egg which you have brushed on.

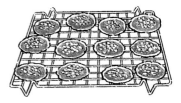

9. Bake the cookies for 15 minutes, until they are golden. Leave them on the trays to cool a little, then lift them onto a wire rack.

Corn flake crunch

Makes 8 pieces

8oz. semi-sweet baking chocolate
3 tablespoons of maple syrup
4 tablespoons margarine
5 cups of corn flakes

an 8-inch shallow, round pan

1. Grease the pan with a little butter or margarine on paper towels. Grease the inside well, but do not use too much butter.

2. Break the chocolate into a large pan. Add the syrup and margarine. Heat the pan gently, stirring all the time.

Lift the pieces out with a blunt knife or a spatula.

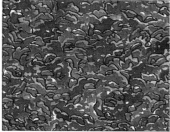

3. When the chocolate has melted, add the corn flakes and stir them well. Make sure that they are coated all over with chocolate.

4. Spoon the mixture into the pan. Gently smooth the top with the back of a spoon. Try not to crush the corn flakes.

5. Put the pan in a refrigerator for the chocolate to set. It will take about two hours. Cut it into eight pieces.

Marshmallow crispies

Makes 15 pieces

4oz. wrapped toffees or slab toffee
½ cup margarine
2 cups marshmallows
7 cups puffed rice cereal

a shallow 11 x 7 inch pan

1. Grease the pan (see page 147). If you are using a slab of toffee, put it in a plastic bag and break it up with a rolling pin.

They will take about 15 minutes to melt.

2. Put the toffee, margarine and marshmallows into a large pan. Melt them very gently over a low heat, stirring all the time.

3. When everything has melted and blended together, take the pan off the heat. Gently stir in the puffed rice cereal.

4. Spoon the mixture into the pan and press it gently with the back of a metal spoon. Leave the mixture to set, then cut it up.

Chocolate chip cookies

½ cup butter or margarine
½ cup sugar
½ cup brown sugar
1 egg
half a teaspoon of vanilla extract
6oz. chocolate chips
1¼ cups flour
½ teaspoon baking soda

Makes 12

1. Grease two large cookie sheets with butter or margarine (see page 147). Turn your oven on to 350°F to heat up.

Use a wooden spoon.

2. Put the white and brown sugar and the butter or margarine into a large bowl. Beat it briskly until it is light and creamy (see page 148).

3. Break the egg into a small bowl and beat it well. Stir in the vanilla, then add the mixture to the large bowl.

4. Sift the flour and the baking soda into the large bowl and stir well to make a smooth mixture. Stir in 4oz. of the chocolate chips.

Press down on each cookie.

5. Put a heaped tablespoon of the mixture onto a cookie sheet. Use up the rest of the mixture to make eleven more cookies.

6. Flatten each cookie slightly with the back of a fork. Sprinkle the top of each one with some of the remaining chocolate chips.

7. Bake the cookies for 10-15 minutes. They should be pale golden brown and slightly soft in the middle.

8. Leave the cookies for a few minutes, then use a spatula to lift them onto a wire rack. Leave them to cool.

Hazelnut cookies

Makes 15

2/3 cup butter or margarine
1/2 cup brown sugar
1/2 teaspoon vanilla
1/4 cup cocoa powder
3oz. chopped hazelnuts or pecans
1/2 teaspoon baking soda
1 1/4 cups flour
1/2 cup sugar
1 egg

You could press a whole nut into the middle of the cookies before you bake them.

1. Follow steps 1-3 of the chocolate chip cookies, using the quantities of ingredients, shown in the list above.

2. Sift the flour and the cocoa powder into the bowl. Use a large spoon to stir it in well, until you get a smooth mixture.

3. Cut the nuts up if necessary, asking an adult for help. Add them to the mixture and stir them in.

Flatten them with the back of a spoon.

4. Put 15 heaped teaspoonfuls of the mixture onto the cookie sheets. Space them out. Flatten each one a little.

5. Bake the cookies for 10-15 minutes. They will darken. Leave them to cool a little, then lift them onto a wire rack.

Shortbread

Makes 8 pieces

1½ cups flour
½ cup butter, refrigerated
¼ cup sugar

an 8-inch shallow pan

1. Turn your oven on to 300°F to heat up. Grease the inside of the pan with butter on a paper towel.

2. Put a strainer over a large mixing bowl and pour the flour into it. Shake the flour into the bowl.

3. Cut the butter into small pieces and put them into the bowl. Mix them with a blunt knife to coat them with flour.

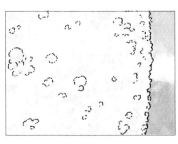

4. Rub the pieces of butter between your fingertips. Lift the mixture and let it fall back into the bowl as you rub (see page 149).

5. Continue rubbing in the flour until the mixture looks like breadcrumbs. Stir in the sugar with a wooden spoon.

6. Holding the bowl in one hand, squeeze the mixture into a ball. The heat from your hand makes the mixture stick together.

Cut across it again, before lifting it out.

7. Press the mixture into the pan with your fingers, then use the back of a spoon to smooth the top and make it level.

8. Use the prongs of a fork to press a pattern around the edge. Then cut the mixture into eight equal pieces.

9. Bake it for 30 minutes, until it becomes golden. Leave the shortbread for five minutes before putting it on a wire rack.

Gingerbread cookies

Makes about 20 cookies

2 cups flour
2 teaspoons of ground ginger
2 teaspoons of baking soda
½ cup butter or margarine
¾ cup soft light brown sugar
¾ cup white sugar
1 egg
4 tablespoons of maple syrup

large cookie cutters

1. Dip a paper towel in some margarine and rub it over two cookie sheets. Turn on your oven to 375°F to heat up.

2. Sift the flour, ginger and baking soda into a mixing bowl. Cut the butter or margarine into chunks and add them.

3. Rub the butter or margarine into the flour with your fingers, until the mixture looks like fine breadcrumbs (see page 149).

Look at the tip for measuring syrup, below right.

4. Stir the sugar into the mixture. Break the egg into a small bowl. Add the syrup to the egg and beat them together well.

5. Stir the eggy mixture into the flour. Mix everything together with a metal spoon until it makes a dough.

6. Sprinkle a clean work surface with flour and put the dough onto it. Stretch the dough by pushing it away from you.

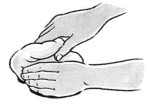

7. Fold the dough in half. Turn it and push it away from you again. Continue to push, turn and fold until the dough is smooth.

158

*You can use
any shape of
cutter you like.*

*Spread the shapes out on
the cookie sheet.*

8. Cut the dough in half. Sprinkle a little more flour onto your work surface. Roll out the dough until it is about ¼in. thick.

9. Use a cookie cutter to cut out lots of shapes from the dough. Lift the shapes onto the cookie sheets with a spatula.

10. Roll out the other half of dough and cut shapes from it. Squeeze the scraps of dough to make a ball. Roll it out and cut more shapes.

Measuring syrup

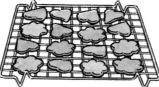

11. Put the cookies on the cookie sheets into your oven and bake them for 12-15 minutes. They will turn golden brown.

12. Leave the cookies on the sheets for about five minutes. Then, lift them onto a wire rack. Leave them to cool.

Heat your spoon in hot water before you measure syrup. It makes it easier for the syrup to slide off.

Oatmeal squares

Makes 12

¾ cup margarine
¾ cup brown sugar
2 tablespoons of corn syrup
2½ cups oatmeal

a shallow 7 x 11 inch pan

1. Put the pan on baking parchment or wax paper and draw around it. Cut out the rectangle just inside the line.

Cut the squares while they are in the pan and still warm.

Grease the pan well.

2. Grease the bottom of the cake pan and put the paper in. Grease the paper. Turn on your oven to 325°F.

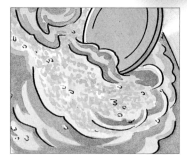

3. Put the margarine in a large pan with the sugar and syrup. Melt the margarine gently. Do not allow the mixture to boil.

4. Take the pan off the heat. Add the oatmeal and stir them in really well so that they are covered in the margarine mixture.

5. Spoon the oatmeal into the pan. Spread them all over the bottom, then smooth the top with the back of a metal spoon.

6. Put the pan on the middle rack in your oven and bake the mixture for 25 minutes until the oats turns golden brown.

7. Take the pan out of the oven and leave it for ten minutes. Cut the mixture into pieces. Leave them in the pan until they are cold.

Chocolate refrigerator cake

Makes about 12 slices

4oz. semi-sweet baking chocolate,
Or, 4oz. white baking chocolate
½ cup butter or margarine
5 tablespoons of corn syrup
8oz. vanilla wafer cookies
2 tablespoons of chopped
maraschino cherries
2 tablespoons of raisins
2 tablespoons of chopped nuts

an 8-inch round pan

Find out how to grease a pan on page 147.

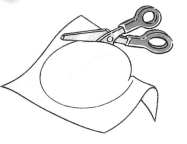

Use white or plain chocolate for this recipe.

1. Put your cake pan onto wax paper and draw around it. Cut out the circle, just inside the line you have drawn.

2. Grease the pan. Put in the wax paper circle you have cut out. Grease it again, on top of the paper circle.

3. Break the chocolate into pieces and put it in a saucepan. Add the butter or margarine and spoon in the syrup.

4. Put the pan over a low heat and let the mixture melt. Stir it occasionally. When the mixture has melted, turn off the heat.

5. Break the cookies into pieces and put them into a bowl. Crush the pieces of cookies finely with a rolling pin or kitchen mallet.

6. Put the chopped cherries, raisins and chopped nuts into the bowl. Add the mixture from the pan and stir well.

7. Spoon the mixture into the cake pan. Press it down really well, then smooth the top with the back of a metal spoon.

8. Put the pan into a refrigerator and leave it overnight. Turn the cake out and pull off the paper. Cut the cake into wedges.

Macaroons

Makes 12

3 large eggs (you only need the whites)
12 whole blanched almonds
1/3 cup sugar
4oz. ground almonds
1/3 cup flour
a few drops of almond extract

Grease the top of the paper.

1. Turn your oven on to 300°F. Cover the cookie sheets with either rice paper or baking parchment.

If you don't have rice paper or baking parchment, cover the cookie sheets with wax paper. Grease the paper lightly.

Be careful not to break the yolk.

You don't need the yolks.

Lift them out with a teaspoon.

2. Break the egg on the side of a bowl. Hold it over a saucer and pull the sides apart. Let the egg fall gently onto a saucer.

3. Hold a small cup over the egg yolk and tip the egg white into a large mixing bowl. Do the same with the other eggs.

4. Put the almonds into the egg white, then lift them out with a spoon. Put them on a plate and leave them on one side.

Make sure your whisk is clean and dry before you begin.

Use a metal spoon to fold the mixture (see the tip, page 183).

5. Beat the egg whites with an electric mixer or whisk until it forms small peaks (see tip, page 173).

6. Add the sugar, ground almonds, flour and almond extract. Fold the mixture over and over gently to mix them.

7. Put a heaped teaspoon of the mixture onto the paper on the cookie sheet, and flatten it slightly with the back of the spoon.

The macaroons spread as they cook.

You can eat any rice paper left on the bottom.

8. Use up the rest of the mixture in the same way, leaving a space between each spoonful. Press an almond onto each one.

9. Bake the macaroons for 25-30 minutes, until they are pale golden brown. Leave them on the cookie sheets for five minutes.

10. Lift the macaroons onto a wire rack to cool. If you have used rice paper, tear away the paper around each macaroon.

Jam cookies

Makes 12 cookies

1½ cups self-rising flour
½ cup butter or margarine
½ cup sugar
1 large egg
1 tablespoon of milk
strawberry jam

You don't have to use strawberry jam; you could try different flavors, such as apricot or plum.

1. Turn your oven on to 400°F. Grease two cookie sheets and sprinkle them with flour. Shake them to spread the flour, then tip off the excess.

2. Put a strainer over a large bowl and shake the flour through it. Cut the butter or margarine into small chunks and add them to the flour.

3. Rub the chunks of butter or margarine into the flour with your fingers, until it looks like fine breadcrumbs (see page 149). Stir in the sugar.

4. Break the egg into a small bowl and add the milk. Whisk them together, then stir them into the mixture in the large bowl.

5. Sprinkle a clean work surface with some flour. Press the mixture together to make a firm ball, then put it onto your work surface.

Don't try to eat them while they are hot. The jam could burn you.

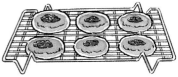

6. Cut the ball in half. Then, cut each half into three pieces. Cut each of the pieces in half. You should end up with 12 even-sized pieces.

7. Squeeze each piece into a round shape and spread them out on the cookie sheets. Make a dent in each cookie and fill it with a teaspoon of jam.

8. Bake the cookies for ten minutes. They will rise and turn golden. Lift each one onto a wire rack and leave them to cool before eating them.

Chocolate choux buns

Makes about 12 buns

⅔ cup cold water
1 teaspoon sugar
4 tablespoons butter
⅓ cup and 1 tablespoon flour
2 eggs

For the filling:
1 cup whipping cream

For the icing:
6oz. semi-sweet baking chocolate
¼ cup powdered sugar

1. Turn on your oven to 400°F. Dip a paper towel in some margarine and rub it over two cookie sheets.

2. Hold each cookie sheet under cold running water Shake them well to get rid of all the drops of water.

3. Put a strainer over a bowl and pour in the flour. Sift the flour into the bowl. Put this on one side. You'll need it later.

4. Put the water, sugar and butter into a large saucepan. Place the pan over a medium heat to melt the butter.

5. As soon as the butter has melted, turn up the heat and bring the mixture to a boil. Then, turn off the heat.

Beat the mixture quickly to mix in all the flour.

6. Immediately, shoot all the flour into the pan at one time, and start to beat the mixture really well with a wooden spoon.

7. Keep beating the mixture until it makes a ball of smooth paste which leaves the sides of the pan clean.

8. Break the eggs into a small bowl and beat them. Add them, a little at a time, beating the mixture each time you add some.

9. Put teaspoonfuls of the mixture onto the cookie sheets. Make sure that they are spaced out. They will spread as they cook.

Slit the buns to allow the hot air inside to escape.

10. Bake them for 25-30 minutes, until they are golden brown. Make a slit in each one and leave them on a rack to cool.

11. Beat the cream until it is stiff. Cut the buns in half. Fill them with a teaspoon of cream, then press them together again.

12. Break the chocolate into chunks and let it melt in a bowl over a saucepan of hot water (see page 149). Stir in the sugar.

13. Using a teaspoon, carefully coat the top of each bun with the melted chocolate. Leave the chocolate to harden.

Scones

Makes 16 scones

1¼ cups self-rising flour
1 level teaspoon of baking powder
a pinch of salt
4 tablespoons butter or margarine
⅛ cup sugar
2oz. raisins
½ cup milk

2½-inch cookie cutter

You can also make fruit scones by adding 2oz. of chopped maraschino cherries or chopped dates, with the sugar at step 3.

Hold the strainer up above the bowl.

1. Turn your oven on to heat up to 450°F. Grease two cookie sheets with butter or margarine on a paper towel.

2. Sift the flour, baking powder and salt into a bowl. Cut the butter or margarine into small pieces and add them to the flour.

Use your fingertips.

3. Rub the butter or margarine into the flour until the mixture looks like fine breadcrumbs. Add the sugar, raisins and milk.

4. Use a blunt knife to mix everything to make a soft dough. Then, press and mold it with your fingers until it's smooth.

5. Sprinkle an area of your work surface with flour and put the dough onto it. Roll it out until the dough is about ½ inch thick.

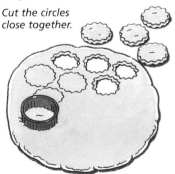

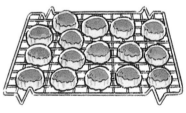

Cut the circles close together.

6. Cut circles from the dough with the cutter. Squeeze the scraps into a ball and roll them out again. Cut more circles.

7. Put the circles onto the cookie sheets, leaving quite a lot of space between each one. Brush the tops with a little milk.

8. Bake the scones for 7-10 minutes on the top shelf of the oven. They will rise and turn golden. Lift them onto a wire rack to cool.

Baked cheesecake squares

Makes 15 squares

1¼ cups flour
½ cup butter
1 tablespoon of sugar
2 tablespoons of water

a 7 x 11 x 1 inch pan

For the filling: 6oz. (⅔ cup) sour cream
8oz. ricotta cheese
¼ cup sugar
a lemon
3 medium eggs
½ cup raisins

Rub in the butter until it looks like breadcrumbs.

1. Draw around the pan on baking parchment or wax paper. Cut out the shape. Grease the pan and put the paper into it.

2. Turn your oven on to 400°F. Sift the flour. Cut the butter into small pieces and rub it in (see page 149).

3. Stir in the sugar. Add the water and mix to make a soft dough. Mix it until the mixture leaves the side of the bowl clean.

Beat the mixture until smooth.

4. Put the dough into the pan and press it with your fingers to cover the bottom of the pan. Press it right into the corners.

5. Prick the dough all over with a fork. Bake it for 10 minutes until it is golden brown. Turn the oven down to 325°F.

6. Put the sour cream, cheese and sugar into a bowl. Grate the yellow rind off the lemon and add it. Beat the mixture well.

Turn the mixture over and over.

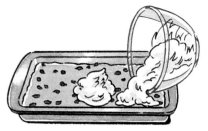

7. Separate the eggs (see page 148). Put the whites into a medium-sized bowl. Add the yolks to the mixture and beat it again.

8. Beat the egg whites until they are stiff (see right). Fold them gently into the mixture with a metal spoon (see page 183).

9. Sprinkle the raisins over the dough and pour the eggy mixture on top. Bake for 45-50 minutes until it is golden brown.

Whisking egg whites

1. Separate the egg whites from their yolks and put them into a clean, dry bowl. Make sure that no yolk gets into the bowl.

2. Hold the bowl tightly in one hand and twist the whisk around and around. The egg will begin to become white and frothy.

3. Continue whisking until the whites get stiff and you get points or 'peaks' forming on the top when you lift up the whisk.

Chocolate brownies

Makes 15

¾ cup margarine
1⅔ cup sugar
1 teaspoon of vanilla extract
3 eggs
1 cup flour
1 level teaspoon of baking powder
1 cup cocoa
6oz. walnuts or pecan nuts

a rectangular pan, 9 x 12 inch

*Use wax paper or
baking parchment.*

1. You will need to grease and flour, or grease and line your pan. If lining, draw around the pan on the paper and cut it out.

2. If you have lined the pan, grease it, then lay the paper in the pan and grease the top of it. Turn the oven on to 350°F.

3. Put the margarine into a pan and melt it over a low heat. Pour it into a large mixing bowl, then add the sugar and vanilla extract.

*Beat the mixture each
time you add some egg.*

4. Break the eggs into a small bowl and beat them. Add them to the large bowl, a little at a time. Beat them in well.

5. Sift the flour into the bowl and add the baking powder and the cocoa. Stir everything together so that it is mixed well.

6. Cut the nuts up, keeping your fingers away from the blade. Add them to the mixture and stir it well again.

7. Pour the mixture into the cake pan and smooth the top with the back of a spoon. Bake it for about 40 minutes.

8. The brownies are ready when they have risen and have formed a crust on top. They should still be soft in the middle.

Use a spatula to lift them.

9. Leave the brownies in the pan for five minutes, then cut them into 15 squares. Leave them on a wire rack to cool.

Pecan squares

Makes 12 squares

For the base: ¾ cup butter or margarine
¾ cup powdered sugar
1¼ cups flour

For the topping: ⅓ cup butter or margarine
2 tablespoons of maple syrup
2 tablespoons of milk
1 teaspoon of vanilla extract
½ cup soft brown sugar
2 eggs
4oz. pecan nuts

a 7 x 11 inch pan

1. Put the pan onto a piece of wax paper or baking parchment. Draw around it and cut out the shape you have drawn.

2. Grease the pan. Put the paper into the bottom of the pan and press it down. Turn the oven on to 350°F.

3. For the base, put the butter or margarine into a mixing bowl. Add the sugar and beat it until it is light and creamy.

4. Sift the flour into the bowl and stir it in well. Sprinkle flour onto a clean work surface and put the mixture onto it.

5. Press the mixture with your fingers, fold it in half, then press again. Do this again and again for about a minute.

6. Use the back of a spoon to press the mixture over the bottom of the pan. Bake it for about 15 minutes or until it is golden brown.

7. When the base has cooked, leave it in the pan, but put it on a wire rack to cool. Begin to make the topping while it cools.

8. Put the butter or margarine into a pan and melt it over a low heat. Stir in the syrup, sugar, milk and vanilla.

9. Break the eggs into a small bowl and beat them well. Take the pan off the heat and stir the beaten eggs into the mixture.

10. Pour the topping onto the base. Sprinkle the pecan nuts evenly over the topping and bake it for about 25 minutes.

11. The topping will turn dark golden brown, but it should be slightly gooey in the middle. Leave it to cool in the pan.

12. When it has cooled, cut it into 12 squares, by making two cuts lengthwise along the pan, then three cuts across.

Banana and nut cake

Makes 9 slices

½ cup butter or margarine
1 cup light brown sugar
2 eggs
2 bananas
⅔ cup self-rising flour
1 teaspoon of baking powder
4oz. chopped nuts

an 8-inch square cake pan

1. Grease your cake pan with butter or margarine on a paper towel. Flour it or line it with paper as on page 179.

2. Turn on your oven to 375°F to heat up. Put the butter or margarine into a mixing bowl. Add the sugar.

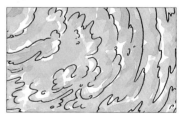

3. Use a wooden spoon to beat the butter or margarine and the sugar, until they are very smooth and creamy.

4. Carefully break the eggs into a small bowl. Beat them with a whisk or a fork until they are mixed well (see page 148).

5. Add the beaten egg to the creamy mixture, a little at a time. Each time you add some egg, beat it into the mixture.

Put the pan on a piece of baking parchment or wax paper which is larger than the pan.

Put the pan on a piece of baking parchment or wax paper which is larger than the pan.

6. Peel the bananas. Put them into a bowl. Mash them well with the back of a fork.

7. Stir the mashed banana into the creamy mixture. Put a strainer over the bowl and sift the flour and baking powder into it.

Use a pencil to draw around the pan, as close to the bottom as you can. Lift the pan off.

8. Use a metal spoon to stir the flour into the mixture. Do this by turning the mixture over slowly with the spoon.

9. Spoon the mixture into your cake pan. Sprinkle the top with the chopped nuts and bake it for about 20-25 minutes.

Cut in from the edge to each corner of the square. Fold in each side along its pencil line.

10. Press lightly on the top of the cake to test it. It should spring back up. Leave it to cool in the pan for five minutes.

11. Lift the cake out by the paper, or turn a floured pan upside down over a wire rack. Leave it to cool, then cut it into slices.

Grease the pan. Fit the paper into the pan. Trim off any extra paper, just above the pan.

Greasing & lining a pan

Simple sponge cakes

Makes 18 squares. Frost the cakes with sugar icing or butter cream frosting.

For the squares: 2 cups self-rising flour
1 cup soft margarine
4 tablespoons of milk
1 level teaspoon of baking powder
1 cup sugar
2-3 drops of vanilla extract
4 eggs

For sugar icing: 1½ cups powdered sugar
about 2 tablespoons of water

For butter cream frosting: ⅔ cup butter, softened
2½ cups powdered sugar
1 teaspoon of vanilla extract

For decorating: candy
a 13 x 9 inch baking pan

Find out about greasing on page 147.

Use a wooden spoon.

1. Grease the pan. Draw around it on baking parchment or wax paper. Cut out the shape and put it in the pan.

2. Turn the oven on to 350°F to heat up. Put a strainer over a large mixing bowl and sift the flour through it.

3. Add the margarine, milk, baking powder, sugar and vanilla. Break the eggs into a small bowl, then add them too. Beat everything well.

Leave the cake in the pan to cool.

4. Scrape the mixture into the pan and smooth the top. Bake it for 40-45 minutes, until the cake springs up when you press the middle.

5. Make the frosting when the cake has cooled. For sugar icing: sift the powdered sugar into a bowl. Add a little water and stir.

Add some more water and stir it again. Continue to do this until the icing coats the back of the spoon and dribbles off it.

For butter cream frosting: beat the butter in a bowl until it is creamy. Sift in the powdered sugar. Add the vanilla and mix it well.

6. Lift the cake out of the pan. Spread the frosting over it. Cut the cake into squares. Decorate them before the frosting sets.

Variations

Cherry and coconut: add 6oz. chopped maraschino cherries and 3oz. shredded coconut to the mixture at step 3.

Chocolate: add 2 tablespoons of cocoa powder to the mixture at step 3. Leave out the vanilla extract.

Lemon: grate the rind off two lemons and add it to the mixture at step 3. Leave out the vanilla extract.

Marble cake

Makes about 8 slices

1 cup butter or margarine
1⅓ cup sugar
4 eggs
1⅓ cups self-rising flour

1 teaspoon vanilla extract
an orange
2 tablespoons of cocoa powder

an 8 x 5 inch loaf pan

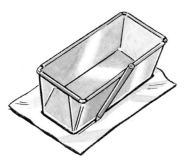

1. You will need to grease and flour or grease and line the pan. If lining, draw around the pan and cut out the shape.

2. Grease inside the pan, then flour it or put your paper in the bottom. Turn the oven on to 350°F to heat up.

3. Put the butter or margarine, vanilla and the sugar into a mixing bowl. Beat them until they are mixed well and creamy.

Beat well each time you add some egg.

4. Break the eggs into a small bowl and beat them. Add the beaten egg, a little at a time, to the creamy mixture.

5. Sift the flour into the bowl, then 'fold' it in with a metal spoon (see tip, right). Divide the mixture between two bowls.

Use the medium holes on your grater.

6. Grate the yellow rind off the orange. Be careful not to grate any of the white part under the skin, as it tastes bitter.

7. Add the orange rind to one bowl and the cocoa powder to the other. Stir each bowl well, using separate spoons.

8. Put alternate spoonfuls of the mixture into the pan. Use a knife to make swirly patterns through the mixture. Smooth the top.

9. Bake the cake for an hour to an hour and 20 minutes. The cake should be well-risen and firm when you press it.

Folding in

You'll see the marble effect when you cut the cake.

10. Leave the cake in the pan for 10 minutes to cool, then turn it onto a wire rack. When it is cold, cut it into slices.

Use a metal spoon to cut through the middle of the mixture, then fold it over very gently. Do this again and again.

Continue cutting and folding until the ingredients are mixed. Folding in keeps your mixture very light.

Layered lemon cake

Makes about 12 slices

a lemon
1¾ cups self-rising flour
1 teaspoon of baking powder
3 eggs
¾ cup soft margarine
¾ cup sugar

For the filling:
2 eggs
½ cup sugar

a lemon
4 tablespoons unsalted butter

For the icing:
a lemon
1 cup powdered sugar

two round 7-inch pans

Heat your oven to 350°F.

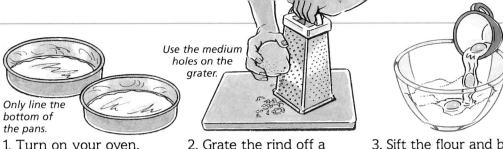

Only line the bottom of the pans.

Use the medium holes on the grater.

1. Turn on your oven. Grease and flour your pans or grease and line your pans with baking parchment or wax paper.

2. Grate the rind off a lemon, then cut the lemon in half. Twist each half on a lemon squeezer to get the juice from it.

3. Sift the flour and baking powder into a bowl. Break the eggs into a cup, then add them, along with the margarine and sugar.

Smooth the top with a spoon.

4. Beat everything in the bowl well, then stir in the lemon rind and juice. Divide the mixture between the two pans.

5. Bake the cakes for 25 minutes until they spring up when you press them in the middle. Leave them on a rack to cool.

6. While the cakes are cooling, make the filling. Break the eggs into a heatproof bowl and add the sugar.

Wear oven mitts.

It will take about 20 minutes.

7. Add the grated rind and juice of another lemon. Cut the butter into small pieces and add it to the bowl.

8. Put some water into a pan and turn on the heat so that the water is just bubbling. Put the bowl into the pan.

9. Stir the mixture from time to time as it thickens. Take it off the heat when it coats the back of your spoon. Leave it to cool.

Leave the cake on the rack.

A zester gives you long pieces of rind.

Press hard as you scrape.

Stir in the juice a little at a time.

10. Spread one cake with the filling. Put the other cake carefully on top. Don't worry if some of the filling oozes out.

11. Either grate some rind from the last lemon or scrape some off with a zester, if you have one. Keep it on one side.

12. Squeeze one half of the lemon. Sift the powdered sugar. Stir in the juice until the icing is like glue. Ice the cake. Sprinkle rind on top.

Apple cake

Makes about 12 slices

1⅓ cups whole-wheat flour
1 cup sugar
1 teaspoon of baking powder
3 eggs
¾ cup soft margarine

1 rounded teaspoon of ground cinnamon
2oz. chopped nuts
1 cooking apple, approx. 8oz.
brown sugar for sprinkling on top

an 8-inch round, loose-bottomed
   cake pan

1. You will need to grease and flour or grease and line your pan. If lining, draw around the pan on the paper and cut out the circle.

2. Grease the pan, then flour it or put the paper circle in the bottom. Turn your oven on to 325°F to heat up.

3. Sift the flour into a large bowl and tip in the grainy pieces left in the bottom of your strainer. Add the sugar and baking powder.

This cake is delicious if you eat it while it is still slightly warm.

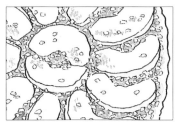

4. Break the eggs into a small bowl, then add them to the bowl along with the margarine, cinnamon and half of the nuts.

5. Use a wooden spoon to mix everything together really well. Spoon the mixture into the pan and smooth the top.

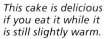

6. Peel the apple (see tip), then cut out the core. Cut the apple into thin slices. Lay the slices in circles on top, overlapping each one.

7. Sprinkle the apples with the remaining nuts and a tablespoon of brown sugar. Bake the cake for an hour, until it is firm.

Peeling apples

Put it on a wire rack to cool.

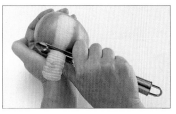

8. Leave the cake in the pan for ten minutes, before slipping off the ring of the pan and lifting the cake off the base. Leave it to cool.

Hold the apple in one hand. Scrape a potato peeler toward you again and again to remove the skin.

Apricot and orange loaf

Makes about 8 slices

4oz. (approx. 1 cup) ready-to-eat dried apricots
an orange
2/3 cup self-rising flour
1/2 cup soft margarine
2/3 cup light soft brown sugar
1/3 cup sugar
2 eggs

For the icing:
1 cup powdered sugar
2 tablespoons of orange juice

an 8 x 5 inch loaf pan

Line the pan with wax paper or baking parchment.

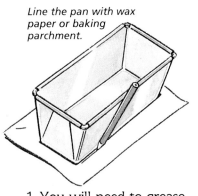

1. You will need to grease and flour or grease and line your pan. If lining, draw around your pan and cut out the shape.

2. Grease your pan and flour it, or grease it and add the paper. Turn your oven on to heat up to 350¡F.

3. Use kitchen scissors to snip the dried apricots into small pieces. Cut them so that they fall into a large mixing bowl.

Use the medium holes on your grater.

Tilt the bowl slightly as you beat.

4. Grate the rind off the orange. Try not to grate any of the white pith underneath. Scrape the rind into the bowl.

5. Sift the flour into the bowl. Add the margarine and sugar. Break the eggs into a cup, then pour them in too.

6. Put the bowl onto a damp dishcloth. Beat the mixture firmly with a wooden spoon, until it is light and fluffy.

7. Scrape the mixture out of the bowl into the loaf pan. Smooth the top with the back of a spoon to make it level.

8. Bake the loaf for about 40 minutes, until it rises and turns golden. Leave it for a few minutes, then turn it onto a wire rack.

Pour on the icing when the loaf is cool.

9. Sift the powdered sugar into a bowl. Mix in some orange juice, a little at a time, until it is like runny glue. Pour it over the loaf.

Chocolate cobweb cake

Makes about 10 slices

2 rounded tablespoons of cocoa
4 tablespoons of hot water
1 cup soft margarine
1 cup sugar
4 eggs
1¾ cups self-rising flour
1 level teaspoon of
baking powder

For the frosting:
8oz. semi-sweet baking
chocolate
½ cup butter
2oz. white chocolate

two 8-inch
round pans

To make a different pattern, do straight lines across the cake and then spread them with a skewer.

Make sure that the circles lie flat.

1. You will need to grease and flour, or grease and line your pans. If lining, put a circle of paper in the bottom of each pan.

2. Turn your oven on to 350°F. Put the cocoa into a small bowl. Add the hot water and mix until it's smooth.

3. Put the margarine, sugar, eggs, flour and baking powder into a large bowl. Beat well, then stir in the cocoa mixture.

Cover the top and the sides.

Smooth the top with a spoon.

4. Put half the mixture into each pan. Bake the cakes for 25 minutes until they rise. Turn them out onto a wire rack to cool.

5. For the frosting, melt the plain chocolate in a bowl over a pan of hot water (see page 149). Cut up the butter and mix it in.

6. Turn one cake flat-side up and spread on half of the frosting. Put the other cake on top. Spread on the rest of the frosting.

Get someone to help you spoon in the chocolate.

7. Break the white chocolate into pieces and put it in a heatproof bowl. Melt it over a pan of hot water. Stir as it melts.

8. Leave the chocolate for five minutes, then take two small plastic bags and put one inside the other. Spoon in the chocolate.

9. Hold the bag over a plate and snip off a tiny corner. Be careful or the chocolate will start to run out immediately.

Tilt the bag between each circle to stop the chocolate from running out.

10. Gently squeeze the bag as you draw a circle in the middle of the cake. Add more circles around it.

11. Drag a skewer or the tip of a knife from the center out to the edge. Do this several times to make a cobweb pattern.

Index

The sign (v) after a page number, means that the recipe is vegetarian. If it has an asterisk (v)* too, the recipe is suitable for vegans (see page 98).

With thanks to Jeanne and Tom Gilbert for their help with the American edition.

This edition first published in 2002 by Usborne Publishing Ltd, Usborne House, 83-85 Saffron Hill,
London EC1N 8RT, England. www.usborne.com Copyright © 2002, 1999, 1998, 1997 Usborne Publishing Ltd.
The name Usborne and the devices are Trade Marks of Usborne Publishing Ltd. All rights reserved.
No part of this publication may be reproduced, stored in a retrieval system, or transmitted in any form or by any means,
electronic, mechanical, photocopying, recording or otherwise, without the prior permission of the publisher.
Printed in Dubai.